Unearthing the Ghosts

To Elizabeth —
Glad we shared
our EMPA
adventure
Linda

Unearthing the Ghosts

a mystery memoir

LINDA MARY WAGNER

Cover design by Joanna Ginsberg
Book design by Jessika Hazelton

Printed in the United States of America
The Troy Book Makers • Troy, New York • thetroybookmakers.com

To order additional copies of this title,
contact your favorite local bookstore
or visit www.tbmbooks.com

ISBN: 978-0-9898220-0-8

Dedicated to

Dr. Joseph Joel Friedman, who convinced me
that my previous doctor had made terrible mistakes.

To my high school teacher Father Bernard Stephan, my sister Carol,
and my childhood friends Chris and Marilyn, each of whom came to
my emotional rescue
at crucial moments that saved my life and turned me toward the
future.

To all those haunted by Anthony A. Sainz
and the drugs he pushed
upon those he deemed "insane."

To my Aunt Leona,
May she rest in eternal peace.

And each separate dying ember
wrought its ghost upon the floor.

~ **The Raven**, Edgar Allan Poe

* * *

ACKNOWLEDGEMENTS

Author Marion Roach Smith and my Troy, New York master class companions, who encouraged me to take my manuscript seriously.

Author Donna Miller and my Troy, New York classmates in Deconstructing Memoir, who pushed me to read many memorable memoirs.

Author Kimberlee Auerbach and my New York City memoir workshop companions, who showed me how each of us can tell our story.

Freelance editor Amie Ruggiero, who cleaned up my manuscript, helped me fine-tune the endnotes, and provided valuable close-to-the-finish-line encouragement.

Freelance editor Brenda Rusch, who provided valuable proofreading and copy editing of the printer's proof.

Author and journalist Robert Whitaker, whose books titled *Mad in America* and *Anatomy of an Epidemic* provided me with an important historical perspective on my own story.

The many songwriters and musicians whose songs have soothed me and helped me understand myself and the world around me throughout my life.

My children, Nathan & Joanna, who have endured years with me as an anxious parent, allowed me to share the outline of this story, and contributed their faith and trust in me. Thanks to Joanna also for her skillful cover design.

Most importantly, my spouse, partner and best friend Barry, who told me when we first became lovers, "No one will ever convince me that you're mentally ill." May it ever be so.

CONTENTS

PROLOGUE

DECEMBER 1969

It was 9 AM during Christmas vacation, just two months after my 17th birthday. None of my five siblings had arrived yet to celebrate the holidays, and I didn't notice that my father had not left home yet for the store, although he was usually gone by 7 AM. My mother walked into my bedroom and asked me to come to the dining room.

"Your father and I have something we want to talk to you about," she said. I could hear from the tone of her voice that it was not going to be good—that they weren't going to ask me what I wanted for Christmas, or where I wanted to go to college next fall.

I had already braced myself for a difficult encounter before Mom led me into the dining room, where my father was seated at his usual "head of the table" seat, and my mother at the other end. When I looked down and saw my diary on the table in front of her, my heart started to race, my face grew hot and my legs seemed paralyzed.

"Sit down," my father said.

I managed to move my body to a sitting position, on the side of the table facing the window. I stared at the outdoors in front of me, searching for a way to escape. Then my mother began, picking up my diary.

"You left this out on your dresser and we are very concerned about what's in it," she began.

Quickly, I turned my head toward her and glared. "How could you read my diary? It's mine, it's private! You wouldn't understand what's in it at all."

My father interjected, "Oh, I think we can understand some of it."

I did everything I could to control myself. This included grasping the sides of the seat on the chair beneath me and not moving one muscle at the risk that I would pick up something and throw it at the window or the wall. I thought about the entries in my diary describing in detail what it felt like to smoke pot for the first time and how I had finally lost my virginity. I also knew that my efforts to evoke a muse to write poetry and to open my mind to new vistas in my diary would appear to my mother and father as incoherent scrawls.

"We don't understand what's been happening to you. We're afraid you're doing things where you'll end up hurting yourself, so we went to talk to the guidance office at school for help."

In other words, I thought, they did not come to me first to discuss my diary entries and ask me questions about what was there or suggest that I go with them to the guidance office. They did not talk to me at all until now.

The principal of Rome Catholic High School was a conservative Papist and a former Marine chaplain, and the guidance officer was another former military man. Here I was, an opponent of the Vietnam War who openly questioned Catholic doctrine about guardian angels in my daily religion class. My parents had turned to this particular school of thought for advice about how to deal with behavior that they had never seen before in any of their older children.

"Father Morelle gave us the name of a doctor and we went to see him," she continued.

"What kind of doctor?"

"He's a psychiatrist who takes care of the nuns when they need counseling. The doctor has reason to believe you've been using drugs laced with some damaging chemicals, and he gave us a prescription for medicine that will counter the effects of these bad drugs."

"Why does he think that? He hasn't talked to me, he hasn't even seen me," I protested, my voice rising, my heart pounding. "How can he prescribe medicine for a patient he hasn't even met?"

"We showed him your diary," my mother answered. "He said he knows what kinds of drugs have been circulating around here. You need to start taking this medicine to avoid the damage from the drugs you've taken."

My mother handed me a large brown vial of prescription medicine. I looked at the label—Trilafon. I didn't know what it was but I knew that if I refused to take it, I could end up like my friend's mother who was sent for electroshock therapy at Marcy State Hospital when she refused to take her meds. By the age of 17, in the era of civil rights battles, anti-war protests and political assassinations, I had learned from the news media that the punishment only gets more severe for those who don't cooperate.

The pills were round with a hard, shiny gray coating, and I was told to take two each, four times per day. As I recollect, I was taking 64 milligrams of Trilafon per day. Today, this is considered the maximum dosage for a raving psychotic adult who is hospitalized and under constant monitoring.

Before the end of January, 1970, I was in the psychiatric ward at St. Elizabeth's Hospital in Utica, N.Y. because the doctor said the medication might affect me more strongly now. Alone in my room there, my vision began to blur, my breasts started to leak milk, I could not summon any type of emotion, and I still had not even met the doctor who had put me there.

My mother had committed me to a psychiatric ward, just as her mother had committed her older sister almost 50 years earlier. But unlike my mother's sister Leona, I had not heard voices, seen hallucinations, nor threatened anyone with harm.

How did this happen? How could my parents do this to me? How can this doctor get away with this? How did I get here? How do I get out? How do I find myself again?

* * *

"How to Find What You've Lost"

Instead of panicking, sit down and think.... Remind yourself of what you were thinking and feeling. Context-dependent memory, in which you put yourself in the same frame of mind, is your best friend right now.

You need to reconstruct the entire scenario mentally, walking through it like a crime scene.

- From an article published January 25, 2011
by Susan Krauss Whitbourne, Ph.D. in *Psychology Today*[1]

I

RETRACING MY STEPS: CHILDHOOD SURVIVAL

SUFFOCATE

AT FOUR AND A HALF, I did not yet know the words "coffin" or "tomb," though I had visited the cemetery with my mom and grandma many times. I had not experienced the death of anything other than ants trapped in a beam of sunlight focused on the sidewalk by a magnifying glass that my brother held on a hot summer day. My brother Richard, at age 12, was not cruel, just curious about the effect of this searing heat on tiny, annoying creatures. At that age, I was curious, too. After kneeling on the grass next to Richard and watching the ants curl up and stop moving, I went searching for other childhood intrigue.

My neighborhood companion, Vivian, showed up at our house to play, giving me another source of entertainment. Soon, the two of us went exploring with my sister Betty, the senior child in charge at the ripe age of eight, and the Sullivan twins, a year younger and a bit smaller than me. This day's adventure would occur in Vivian's garage attic, a wondrous store of hidden treasures. Just a bit older than me, Vivian was not allowed to play in the attic, but that didn't stop us from climbing up the ladder and stepping inside.

The light in the attic was dim since the only window up there was blocked. Old furniture and boxes were stuffed in and piled so high that it was difficult for the five of us to maneuver through the space. We made our way to a large, clothing-storage trunk with a dusty black exterior and a big brass lock on the center. Betty opened the top and coughed from the dust until she saw what lay inside.

"Wow! What a great hat," she said as she pulled out a ladies' dark red felt hat with pink and white silk roses along the brim. She put it on and used a fake British accent. "Shall we go to the market today?"

Vivian pulled out a pair of black leather ice skates with double blades. "I wonder if these will fit me," she said, trying to pull them on over her sneakers. One of the twins pulled out a long black stick with a white tip.

"It's a magic wand!" Betty said. "Let's pretend we're in a magic show!"

"How do we do that?" I asked.

"You and Vivian climb inside the trunk. I'll be the magician," Betty planned. "When I say abracadabra, one two three, you pop out like magic."

"My mom won't let me do that," Vivian whined.

"Your mom doesn't even let you be in here, but you're here, aren't you?" Betty prodded.

When Vivian started to cry louder, "I don't want to," Betty said, "OK," knowing she'd been defeated. "Linda and the twins will go in the trunk."

As a pensive and somewhat passive child, I obeyed my sister's wishes and climbed into the trunk along with the Sullivan sisters after Betty emptied it. Once inside, they lowered the top and as the dim light disappeared from view, I heard a small "click."

With that sound, the walls seemed to close in as darkness descended. I heard Betty's muffled voice say something like, "Through the mystery of magic, we will now make three little girls appear! Abracadabra, one, two, three!"

I pushed up on the roof of the trunk, but it wouldn't budge.

I heard Betty again, louder this time, "Abracadabra, one, two, three!"

I pushed harder and told the twins to push too, and even though one tried to help me, the top stayed shut.

"I can't get out!" I yelled to my sister, anxiety rising in my voice.

I heard Betty and Vivian struggling to open the top. The sound of metal scraping was followed by an even louder click than it made when Betty first closed the top. I pushed with all my might, but it still wouldn't move.

The twins had already started crying, and their tears were contagious. "Let me out, let me out!" I screamed in a fever pitch.

"I'm trying, I'm trying. Don't cry. It will be OK."

But I could hear the fear in my sister's voice as she said to Vivian, "You stay here, I'll go get my mom."

Then I heard Vivian in a weak voice, "Don't cry now. I'll sing you a song." She began singing, "Row, row, row your boat gently down the stream. Merrily, merrily, merrily, merrily, life is but a dream." When she got to the second round, I started to sob inconsolably.

I was hot with my own body heat and that of the twins, drenched in my own sweat and tears, my thin body tucked into that cramped space. I was no longer fully conscious of the twins' presence, unaware of anything but my own desire to breathe the air, to break out and see anything other than horrible black darkness.

Betty didn't know Vivian's family very well, but she knew they had forbidden Vivian and her friends to play in the garage. So, instead of just running inside Vivian's house where her mother and grandmother remained blissfully ignorant of our dilemma, Betty ran down the block to our house for help.

After a few more minutes, Vivian stopped singing. I stopped sobbing and started praying the Hail Mary that Betty had taught me. "Hail Mary," I whispered, "full of grace, heaven art thou among women and blessed is the fruit of thy womb Jesus." I bowed my head briefly at his name. I had to pee but held it, although I could smell the dark musky odor coming from the twins who were still crying.

I heard and felt the vibrating footsteps on the attic stairs, the raised voices getting closer and closer. And then I heard my mother say, "Lin, hold on. We're here. We're going to get you out of there." Then she yelled, "Dick, over there. You can use that."

Next I heard and felt something like a hammer smash the trunk right in front of my nose. Another whack, and another, and suddenly a crack of dim light grew to a rush of air. I gulped it down. I don't recall much about getting out of the trunk, beyond that feeling of air rushing past my face, into my windpipe and lungs. I don't recall whether anyone hugged or kissed me, just the sudden, overwhelming ability to breathe.

Years later, I learned that my brother had used an axe to smash the lock. And my mother when telling the story would always say, "You never saw anyone get out of a place so fast."

My brother had saved my life. Was this the same young man who fried ants on the sidewalk? The same one who ran away when I was born, because I was just another girl like his other four sisters? Was this Richard, who routinely took my arm and forced me to slap myself in the face? The same brother who jumped on me when I sat quietly on the couch, reading a comic book, and held a pillow over my face while I screamed, "Mom, he's trying to suffocate me!"

And he would yell, "She's just trying to get me in trouble."

Yes, this was the very same brother, whom I came to idolize after he broke that lock and got me out alive.

I never blamed Betty, whom I idolized for different reasons. But she was left feeling shame and guilt for decades, after Mom's weighty words to her later that day, "How did you let that happen?"

Attics can be wonderlands, offering windows into a past filled with old shoes and hats, buckles and coins, and odd, ancient wind-up toys set aside for tomorrow's grandchild. The boxes stacked there can cast shadows that provoke imaginations young and old to see and hear ghosts, intruders and monsters where there are none.

But in Vivian's garage attic, fear was warranted and horror was as palpable as the water that could be wrung from my shirt when I finally emerged with the twins into the stale attic air. For years afterward, I had nightmares of a tall, dark specter in a black cape and hood rising up from behind attic boxes. I would awaken in a startled sweat, my heart racing and my breathing strained.

CHOKE

WITH HER LONG BROWN HAIR, CHUBBY torso, and eccentric habits that included talking to an imaginary friend, Vivian was taunted repeatedly by the Rhodes boys, whose house was settled between the two of ours.

"Vivian, the wonder horse. Vivian, the wonder horse," they chanted in unison whenever she came onto the scene. The boys would hang around with me, but not with her.

Vivian lived with her mother, grandmother and older sister. Her father, deceased, had left them with a comfortable life, which was clear to me when I saw the large collection of beautiful dolls and doll clothes in the bedroom that was hers alone. Although our approach to play differed by a long shot, Viv was the only female companion my age in the neighborhood. With so many older sisters, including Betty who was just four years older than me, I did not long for girlfriends. Of course, my sisters were always happy when they could leave me unattended with a playmate rather than having me tag along with them. Vivian had just one sister, ten years older, and she was much hungrier for a girl pal who was still interested in toys.

I would have preferred to run down to the playground and hop on a swing, kick a ball, or practice cartwheels in the grass. But Vivian had a more sedentary, Victorian imagination. Many of our interactions revolved around eating.

One of our favorite past-times was making a picnic lunch of Wonder Bread peanut butter and grape jelly sandwiches at a table made from cardboard boxes and set in the sandbox outside my back door. Viv would pretend to be a British lady at high tea, serving me grape-flavored Kool-Aid from a ceramic pitcher poured into paper cups.

Another favorite activity we shared was sitting on the curb at the corner, beyond which we were not allowed to venture. We would scout for whatever we could see from that last vantage point, eager for the day when we could walk across the street. One warm summer day in 1957, we sat there together with a special treat: two pieces of hard, round butterscotch candy that Vivian's mother had given to her to share with me.

In a poor neighborhood, butterscotch candy was a rare luxury. I took my time unwrapping the clear, golden yellow wrapper and deeply breathed in the delicious scent of the candy. Just as I put it in my mouth, Vivian made a funny snorting noise and silly face. As I gasped in laughter, I inhaled that entire hard, round butterscotch candy directly into my windpipe.

As the pain pierced my throat and chest and panic hurled me upward, I flew through the air toward home, not understanding what was happening as my feet barely skimmed the surface of the ground. I burst through the front screen door into the living room, where my mother stood cleaning up a spill. The door, with its rickety wooden frame and squeaky hinges, made so much noise that Mom turned around immediately.

My mother knew how to diagnose and fix mechanical things, and I was about to become as mechanical as a vacuum cleaner. She took one look at me, now blue in the face, lips the color of ash, and in one swift, smooth move, grabbed me by the leg and arm and turned me entirely upside down. She whacked me in the center of my back, and that perfectly round golden butterscotch shot out of my mouth and skipped across the floor.

"You're all right now, you're all right now," she said, and rubbed my back as I sobbed. "The candy just got stuck in your throat, but it's gone now, and you're all right."

But that night, as I lay in bed, I was startled awake in the midst of a new repeating nightmare—a car, in which I ride in the front passenger seat, drives off the edge of a black, steel bridge, and I am falling, falling, falling until splat! I awake again, sweat dripping down my forehead. My child's mind could tell I was alive and it was just a bad dream, but the luminescent crucifix on the wall opposite my bed startled me into thinking there was a ghost hovering in my room.

I DROPPED YOU ON YOUR HEAD

A COUPLE YEARS AFTER THE BUTTERSCOTCH incident, a television entered our living room and forever altered the dynamic of our family conversations. The room was already crowded with enough furniture to seat only eight of the ten of us who lived together in my grandma's three-bedroom, 100-year-old house. With just one bathroom for ten people, the house was a lesson in patience, tolerance and the efficient use of space.

The glow from our very first wooden console black-and-white TV set cast an eerie light on my mother's face while a summer thunderstorm crashed and flashed outside our windows. Mom stood at the ironing board, pressing Dad's shirts, while the early-afternoon soap operas lured her to a distant escape from her housewife doldrums in 1960.

"To live each day for whatever life may bring…this is *Love of Life*," the TV voice box boomed in a deep, masculine voice from the woven-straw speaker cover.

Dressed in hand-me-down pink sleeveless shirt and shorts, my straight brown hair in a summertime pixie cut, I sat on the worn sofa across from my mother with our family photo album on my lap. Sepia-toned photos from the 1920s were stuck into corners on worn, black-paper pages inside a thick, black faux-leather cover. At eight years old, I saw the album as a window to ancient history.

Suddenly, the sweeping sound of an organ playing the *Love of Life* theme song filled our living room while an image of the Plaza Hotel in New York City, far from our little upstate village, popped onto the screen.

"No, Meg, no!" the TV screamed. "How can you do this to me?" the beautiful young actress shouted at her soap sister, who stood in a hallway, her arms wrapped around a handsome man.

My mother set the iron down and held my father's shirt limply in her hand while she stared at the TV.

"Gloria, it's over. He loves me now," the other lovely actress spit in harsh tones, her eyes flashing like the lightning outdoors.

I compared my mother, standing in front of me, to the much slimmer image of her in the photo on my lap. She appeared fit and slender, teetering on a rock by the edge of a lake, holding the hand of a familiar young man with a big grin on his face. After a closer look, I could tell it was a young Frederick, who was now my dad. As I flipped through the pages, I was jolted by a sudden fear and vision.

"Mom. Mom!" I shouted, but she didn't turn from the TV. "I remember something scary. I remember being on a cold table, shiny and hard." My face crumpled up, worry lines creasing my forehead.

My mother was now transfixed by a commercial for a new type of laundry detergent.

"Mom, I can see a machine over my head. It looks like the inside of our TV set. Or, or, like a flying saucer." My lean, bean-pole body jiggled with nervous energy. "Mom! Mom, did you hear me?" I blurted. But she was still looking at the TV, not at me, watching her "stories," as she called the daytime soaps.

"I remember the room. It was quiet and cold and you're there Mom, with someone in all white next to you."

"What, dear?" she finally roused out of her fog as the show ended and a station break came on the air. I started my story all over again. As she returned her attention to the ironing, she finally heard me when I said, "You and a doctor were there together. You look like you're talking, but I can't hear anything. I think I've gone deaf!"

"Are you sure you didn't dream this, dear?" she asked, slowly putting one finished shirt on a hanger.

"No, it's not like a dream, I remember it. I remember it like it really happened, Mom."

"Well," she said, flipping another shirt around to press the sleeve, her voice tinged with surprise. "I suppose you may be remembering the X-ray."

"X-ray? For what?"

"Well you were only two, but maybe you could remember it. You had an X-ray after I dropped you on your head."

"You dropped me on my head?" I said incredulously.

The silence between us was filled by the sound of my favorite TV commercial.

"N.E.S.T.L.E.S., Nestlé's makes the very best...chooooc-late."

"Why, Mom? How did you drop me on my head?" I asked in a slightly accusatory tone.

"Well, I took you with me shopping downtown in Syracuse," she said, keeping her eyes focused on her work. "We didn't have a car, so I had to take the bus. I was holding you and the shopping bags, wearing a straight skirt, and when I stepped up to get on the bus, I slipped. The skirt was too tight and I was just trying to juggle too much," she added, now looking over at me. "I lost my balance and you fell out of my arms, right onto your head on the cement curb."

She looked down at her ironing again.

"Oh no!" I yelled. "Did I split my head open?"

"I should not have worn that skirt when I had to carry you," she said quietly, her voice shaking.

"Did I get bloody?"

"Grandma was so upset with me when we got home," she said. Her face was turning crimson.

"Did my brains come out on the ground?"

"No, no. You were just knocked unconscious," she answered at last, pricking the balloon of my morbid excitement. "An older couple with a car stopped, and they drove us to the emergency room at the hospital. The doctor said you had a concussion. I just had to make sure you stayed awake after you came to."

A concussion. *Wow*, I thought, *that sounds serious*.

"That explains why you're such a weirdo," yelled my brother from the next room. At 16, Richard saw it as another golden razzing opportunity and he taunted, "You're damaged goods."

ESCAPE THE FALLING BRANCH

By the time I was six and in first grade, all of my three oldest sisters were in high school.

Joan, the eldest, had survived spinal meningitis and rheumatic fever just as antibiotics and vaccines were becoming available in the 1940s and '50s, but they left her spine crippled with severe scoliosis. Around the time that I was an infant, Joan was about twelve and had to spend a year in a body cast in the hospital to ensure that her body would not be permanently twisted into the shape of a pretzel that pulled her neck toward her lower back. She survived it all as an "A" student with dark hair, large, dark eyes and a sweet smile and angelic personality. By 1958, she was about to graduate and head up the hill to the local Jesuit College.

Miraculously, Joan was the only child in our crowded home who fell so seriously ill. Nevertheless, her sickness focused and sapped an extensive amount of our mother's maternal energies. My sisters Joan, Carol and Diane and my brother Dick all benefited from the fact that we lived with my grandmother, who was still physically capable of being the backup mom during their childhoods.

Joan had been born in March 1940, Carol in May 1941, and Diane in October 1942. My parents slowed down after that, with my brother born in August 1944 and my sister Betty in February 1948.

So it's not surprising that by 1952, when I was conceived and born, my mother had little time to give me the motherly affection I needed. Dealing with a serious medical condition in her eldest child and with the maintenance of four others under the age of twelve, she had to prop up a bottle of formula in my crib rather than hold me while I was fed. However this may have affected my emotional or physical development, it was counterbalanced by the attentions—both positive and negative—of five older siblings who saw me at various times as their own baby doll to coddle and comfort, or rival sister to be taunted and teased.

Research shows that the children of more involved parents hear about 20 million more words before they enter kindergarten than the children of neglectful parents. In my case, I was fortunate to have loquacious, bright older siblings who poured words into my ears from the moment I was born until they gradually left home to make their own ways in the world. My sister Diane even drilled me over dinner with questions raised in her Philosophy 101 class, "Linda, how do you know you exist? How can you prove it? Is knowledge knowable, and if so, how?"

The other major influences on my development were the Franciscan Sisters who taught me at St. Matthew's. Heading up to the far end of Heman Street to half-day kindergarten was both exciting and terrifying. I had to mix in with more than 50 other children at tables in a large open room, and use a bathroom toilet that sounded like jet planes lifting off when you flushed. For the first week, I wet my pants rather than use that commode and risk falling in and drowning in the swirl. I would run home at lunchtime to change quickly, hiding my undies beneath my bed in the hope that my mother wouldn't notice.

Sister Mary Lambert was my kindergarten teacher, and she loved to have us march around the room at least once a week to the sound of music from the record player, while we hummed on kazoos, clanged on triangles, or shook tambourines. Since she was a good friend of one of the fourth-grade teachers, Sister Elizabeth John, they occasionally combined the kindergarteners and 4th graders for a half-hour entertainment session. During one of those sessions, right after Chubby Checker's "The Twist" hit the charts, Sister Elizabeth John put the 45 rpm black vinyl record on to play and told the 5-year-old and 9-year-old students to show how the twist is done. I must have appeared eager but shy, so Sister Mary Lambert picked up the yardstick and shook it at me and shouted, "C'mon Wagner, you know how to do it. Get out there and twist!" Being more afraid of her loud voice and the snap of the yardstick, I twisted as hard and long as I could, until I started giggling and feeling right at home.

By the time I got to first grade, I had received intellectual coaching for several years from my three eldest sisters, all of whom were top students. That year, my teacher at St. Matthew's was Sister Mary Krista, a young, angelic-faced Franciscan nun who was assigned the "A" class of 52 pupils. I clearly recall standing up in front of our class and impressing her by spelling a word my sister Diane had drilled into me. "A-N-T-I-D-I-S-E-S-T-A-B-L-I-S-H-M-E-N-T-A-R-I-A-N-I-S-M. Antidisestablishmentarianism!" I shouted out. I had no idea what it meant, but at age six, I could spell it.

Our school, recently constructed, was a kindergarten through 8th grade Catholic school that had not been available for my older siblings, who had attended the Heman Street public elementary school and East Syracuse High School before it merged with Minoa. Our small Catholic parish had one of the most beautiful stone churches graced by remarkable stained glass windows this side of the Atlantic. When I was a kid, it was led by Father

Bennett, a deep-voiced, silver-haired and strict but kind, gentle priest—a real-life incarnation of the type of compassionate clergyman that actor Spencer Tracy could only pretend to be.

One day, I was alone, making the two-block walk to school after a heavy storm the night before. I had just crossed the street when an enormous branch fell from the large old oak tree whose branches spread across the entire intersection. It crashed to the ground just a foot behind me as I passed beneath the tree's crown. I stopped in my tracks and as I looked back with startled alarm, my heart raced and I gulped a breath of air. Then I continued on my way to school, while doors in the neighboring houses opened and heads peeked out to see the cause of the explosive sound.

I forgot about the entire thing until I got home that afternoon. I tried to tell my mother about it, but she was busy cleaning up and since I was not hurt, it was just another child's tale. But when my father got home in the evening, I ran to tell him about my latest close call. As always, he picked me up in his arms and I patted him on the back. In religion class at school, I was learning that people like my father, who were not baptized Catholic, would burn in hell eternally. But I could not imagine that this big, gentle man who always smiled at me when he came home and who comforted me when I was hurt or afraid could really deserve to burn forever. I thought that God must make exceptions for good people who didn't do everything the priests and nuns thought they should do.

* * *

Religion class at St. Matthew's focused on the catechism and the lives of the saints. Unlike the practice of evangelical Christians, there was little Bible study. However, there was much preaching about the dangers of Communism during the late 1950s to mid-1960s in Catholic schools.

One of the free reading treats that we received at St. Matthew's was a Catholic comic book series titled *Treasure Chest of Fun and Fact*. *Treasure Chest* was filled with entertaining cartoons, word puzzles, tales of the early Christians, and retold Greek myths, alongside stories about sports heroes. These "Highlights" for Catholic kids also included moral lessons, Catholic dogma, and in the early 1960s, a series on "This Godless Communism," was introduced by a letter to young readers from FBI Director J. Edgar Hoover.[2]

The series on communism told an abbreviated history of the march of this ideology, starting in Russia and moving on through a series of domino nations that fell under its evil spell. The ultimate message was that the FBI needed to monitor Americans who were suspected of communist sympathies and that unless we fought a communist conspiracy and takeover, children would turn on their parents, churches would be closed, and we would lose the right to vote. It was a powerful medium to tell such a frightening story to children, and I was especially vulnerable to its tale spinning.

As a result, around the age of ten, I began to look for those who might be communist spies within my own circle of family, friends and teachers. In the early mornings, when I first awoke in my top bunk bed, I would lie quietly in bed and look around the room. On many mornings, I would see my grandma lying still in the bed below, watching me. But when I glanced down at her, she would quickly close her eyes. While I'm sure now that she was just playing with me, I thought she was spying on me, and came to the conclusion for several months that my grandmother must be a communist.

FAINT

EAST SYRACUSE HAD A FEW FINANCIALLY comfortable families during the 1950s and '60s—the Klines, who were undertakers, and the village dentist among them. But the vast majority of families in our village were working poor, some with less than others.

Janet was one of the girls in my class whose family had even less than mine, despite the fact that she was an only child while my parents had the additional expense of five other children along with me. Her skin was pasty white and her arms were bony stretches of skin; her small head was topped with plentiful, fine, pale brown hair. Since she lived two blocks further from St. Matthew's than me, she usually walked up my block to get to school. At the age of eight, when we were in second grade, Janet and I began walking home together. A strange bond formed between us, glued together by religious imagery we encountered daily during our instruction in Catholic dogma.

When we played at Janet's home, we would often dress up the shrine she kept to the Virgin Mary. The statue of Mary was only about four inches high, made of a tan plastic with no color painted on it. Janet made a backdrop for the shrine from a cardboard box, the inside of which was draped with a flowered scarf. In the warmer weather, we would pick wildflowers for the shrine, weaving lilies of the valley into a tiny crown to place upon Mary's head or at her feet if the circle was too large to stay on her head. We'd set violets into a shot glass that Janet found in her kitchen cupboard.

One day Janet asked me to go to her house after school because she wanted to show me a great treasure that she had been gathering for her shrine. She told me she had precious jewels that were worth a great deal of money. When we got to her house, we went to her bedroom, where the shrine stood atop a tall dresser that was missing a drawer. She quietly looked down the hallway to make sure her mother and father were not coming, and then she drew the curtain that separated her room from the hall, and disappeared underneath her bed. In a few minutes, she crawled back out with a tin that used to hold tobacco, and when she opened it, the strong smell of tobacco filled the air. Inside were the precious jewels—small, shiny pieces of faceted glass, plastic beads, rhinestones, and sequins that may have come off an old dress, scarf, or costume jewelry. There were smooth pieces of glass that had probably come from pieces of broken bottles worn smooth by the running water of a stream or river. Some of the pieces appeared to be buttons. But to both of us, these were indeed rare treasures that belonged in the precious company of Mary and her shrine. We planned to talk to Sister Mary Krista about getting some paste from the school supply the next day, so that we could glue the jewels onto the walls inside the shrine box.

Sister Krista was, of course, happy to see two girls engaged in creating a shrine to the Blessed Virgin, and she readily agreed. She found a paper cup to hold some of that thick white paste that smelled so slightly of mint that many children younger and hungrier than us would eat it as if it were candy. Over the next several weeks, we worked on the shrine after school, stringing some of the beads and sequins on thread to hang from the top of the box, and gluing some of the rhinestones, glass jewels and buttons along the bottom and sides of the box.

When we ran out of our precious stones, we thought that this shrine must be the most beautiful and valuable shrine in the entire world. We would pull down the curtains and turn off the lights in the room and shine a flashlight to see the shrine sparkle. Then we would say prayers, asking for good things for our families, and for new toys like bikes, dolls and board games.

After we grew bored with the shrine, we began to stay at my house after school. In the first hour or so, the only other family members at home were my mother and grandmother, who were always busy downstairs or outdoors with laundry, cooking, cleaning, or gardening. My older sisters were at their college classes; my brother was working after school and my sister Betty was at cheerleading practice. My father and Uncle Glenn were at work, so Janet and I would have the entire upstairs to ourselves.

I always preferred to spend that time in the bedroom that my three older sisters shared. They had chosen the color lavender to paint the walls, and they had found fabric with a white background covered with tiny lavender flowers and green leaves to make curtains for the windows and closet. To my mind, this was the prettiest room in the house, even though it was stuffed with three twin beds, a dresser and a closet filled with "big girl" clothes.

One day, Janet told me about a special fainting game. She told me to go behind her and put my arms around her stomach just below her ribs, with my hands clasped tightly together. She showed me where to place my clasped fists and then told me to squeeze my arms tight and pull in my fists quickly. I did as she said, and within a couple of minutes, her face got white, her arms and legs went limp and she slid down to the floor, her eyes closed. At first I was terrified and ran to the bathroom to get some cold water to splash on her face. By the time I got back, she was sitting up on the floor, her eyes wide open and her face pink.

"Where did you go?" she asked as I gave her the paper cup of water.

"I went to get this," I said. "I thought you might be dead."

She laughed. "I just fainted. You see, that's the trick. See how it works?"

"That's scary!"

"It's fun," she insisted. "You should try it. It's your turn now."

"I don't know. Does it hurt?"

"No, you feel as light as a feather. Then you fall down. You know, 'we all fall down!' like ring around the rosy?"

"Well, I guess I'll try it just once," I said with some trepidation.

"Okay," said Janet, hopping back up on her feet. "Turn around."

Janet got me in the same lock-hold that I had put her in a few minutes before. She squeezed and squeezed until I was about to shout, "That's enough," but the words wouldn't come out of my mouth. Suddenly, the air was all gone from my lungs, my head felt like a feather and I floated away.

Some time later, I woke up and Janet was looking through the sweaters stacked in my sisters' closet. I had a little headache, but I was still alive.

We repeated this game a couple more times until I had a bad headache which I can still feel when I recall this scene from my past. I looked at the clock and it was four o'clock, the time when Janet would head home.

"I have to do my homework now," I said.

"I have to walk home and get the food out to start dinner," Janet responded.

"You cook dinner?"

"My mom is working now, so I get supper started for her. Maybe sometime you could come over and eat supper with us."

The thought of eating at anyone else's house was frightening to me in general. But I felt especially strange about eating supper that was cooked by someone my own age.

"OK, maybe," I said, although I knew I would always find a reason not to accept this dinner invitation.

"OK, bye," Janet said, and we walked downstairs together.

No one in my family or at school ever found out about the fainting game that Janet and I played every so often. That evening it was a little harder than usual to concentrate on my homework and I had to do more pages over than usual. But I finished it all, and like usual, I earned gold stars and little angel stamps on the homework I turned in the next day at school.

Linda Mary Wagner, age 7, dressed for First Communion

St. Matthew's Church in East Syracuse, NY

Father Bennett, pastor of St. Matthew's Church in the 1950s and '60s.

Linda and her siblings 1958 - from top left, Richard/"Dick", Betty,
2nd row Carol, Diane, Joan, Linda (on Diane's lap)

Linda with neighborhood friend Vivian

II

RETRACING FAMILY STEPS:
DISCOVERING JOY & TRAGEDY PAST

HOLIDAY TREASURES

WONDERFUL SENSATIONS SURROUNDED THE HOLIDAYS IN our home when I was a child. As children and teenagers, we don't always recognize how such traditions are a family's gift to us that can serve as comforting memories in times of future distress.

The Christmas season began with anticipation oozing from my handwritten note to Santa that listed hopes and dreams for toys, sweets and blessings of all types. In our family, this list was never written before Thanksgiving. Today's stores start decorating and advertising for Christmas sales as soon as Halloween masks and costumes are put away. But in the mid-to-late 1950s in my family and neighborhood, the sights and sounds of each season were clearly delineated by family rituals peculiar to each holiday that were not drowned out by commercial clatter.

Just before Halloween, my mother, grandmother and all six children were busy in the kitchen heating a sweet molasses and corn syrup concoction and popping popcorn. The popcorn was cooked in a large, heavy, metal pot whose orange cover was topped by a wooden crank that turned a curly-cue bar inside. This bar would sweep the popcorn kernels through the hot oil until the popping had passed beyond a fast, frenzied noise and fluffy white bursts began to push the cover off the pan. After a huge bowl was filled, Mom brought over the heated dark-brown syrup and poured it over the popped corn, mixing it all with a huge ladle.

The job of most of the kids was to wash our hands before immersing them into this sticky mixture and grab enough pop-corn to roll into a ball the size of a good, packed snowball. We sat around the heavy, rectangular metal kitchen table, which had a white top bordered in red. A couple kids had the job of ripping sheets of waxed paper off the roll, and wrapping the gooey pop-corn balls up into packages that could be dropped into the open bags of trick-or-treaters on Halloween night.

From the earliest ages, we planned our costumes and made them from whatever was available. One year, I burned a cork to make charcoal whiskers on my face to look like the many hobos who came from the railroad yards to our back door, and I put some of my sister's red lipstick on my nose to make it look like a drunkard's schnozz. A red bandana stuffed with newspaper was tied onto a stick from the back yard, so I could sling it over my shoulder as if those were my only earthly possessions. My sweat-shirt was stuffed with more newspaper to make it look like I had a beer belly, and my own clothes were covered by an old, moth-eaten wool jacket that my father was going to throw out.

The treats in our neighborhood included invitations into an open garage for heated apple cider and homemade donuts. People still gave children homemade candied apples in those days, before some sicko inserted single-edged razor blades into apples that kids found in their bags, or at least that's what the urban legend says.

After the days of hayrides, bonfires, scarecrows and carved pumpkins were over, things went back to normal until a few days before Thanksgiving, when Mom and Grandma began to plan and prepare the holiday meal. Dad brought home fresh cranberries that would be cooked into sauce while Mom set aside bread to dry out to make sure she'd have the fixings for stuffing.

On the day before the feast, Dad would bring home an enormous turkey and there was always discussion about how to ensure that no one would get sick from a bird stuffed too early or kept too warm before it was fully cooked.

On Thanksgiving Day, each of us had a specific job. One job was to help with preparing the fresh fruit salad that went into the special crystal goblets used only on Thanksgiving and Christmas. Grapes were an essential part of this dish, and these were the days before seedless grapes were widely available. So, one of my jobs was to wash the grapes, slice them down the center, and remove the seeds.

Although we did not usually say a prayer before dinner, on Thanksgiving we always said grace before the feast. As soon as I was old enough to remember the prayer, it was my job as the youngest to say, "Bless us, O Lord, and these thy gifts which we are about to receive from thy bounty, through Christ Our Lord."

And everyone answered, "Amen."

My brother Dick would say soon after that, "Rub a dub dub, thanks for the grub. Yay, God!" We would all laugh and dishes and silverware began to clink as we dug into our food.

After the Thanksgiving leftovers were eaten and all the special holiday dishes put away, it was time to make a list for Santa. I made my list knowing I could not get everything I requested, but hoping against all odds that my most desired objects would appear under the Christmas tree. Since giving was an important part of the tradition, I saved my pennies, nickels, dimes and quarters to make sure I'd have enough to get small gifts for Mom, Dad, and Grandma. Usually, this meant handkerchiefs or socks from Sacks' Five and Dime store on Main Street. I was not expected to get gifts for my five siblings.

In the week before Christmas Day, a huge box would arrive on our front doorstep from Aunty Jo, Grandma's sister. She lived too far away to join us, and she had her own adopted daughter who was older than my oldest sisters. But she always sent this special box that included many small wrapped gifts for each of us. The best part of Aunty Jo's package was the element of surprise. Nothing that she sent was on our wish list.

The most memorable tradition of the winter holiday season in our family was the music. Everyone in our family had a pleasant singing voice, an ability to harmonize and stay in key, and knowledge of the lyrics to nearly every Christmas song ever written. All three of the oldest girls had taken piano lessons and we had a big old upright in the front room where the Christmas tree was set up. In the days before Christmas, while we wrapped presents, prepared food for Christmas dinner, got the nativity crèche and its tiny statues of Mary, Joseph and Baby Jesus out of the closet, or decorated the house and tree, the holiday tasks were suffused with four-part harmony. Our rendition of songs like "O Holy Night" or "O Come, O Come, Emmanuel" was filled with deep spiritual and emotional feeling, while "Frosty the Snowman" was just for fun.

Singing was an ingredient in our Christmas cookies—the simple sugar cookies that we made together, rolling out chilled dough for hours, and cutting it into the shape of snowflakes, Santa, stars, candles and fir trees. After sliding the cookie sheets into the oven, waiting for the cookies to cool was the hardest part of this tradition, because I just itched to decorate and then eat them. We'd coat the cooled baked treats with a multi-colored frosting mixture of powdered sugar and milk, topping the frosting off with red and green sugar crystals, rainbow-colored nonpareils, red cinnamon dots and chocolate speckles. This ritual, involving all of us in the kitchen, was central to the Christmas season.

Early in the morning on Christmas Day, we came downstairs to find a beautifully lit tree covered with the same old ornaments each year, sparkling with silver icicles, and hovering over a corner filled with gift-wrapped packages. Some years might have more packages than others, but there was always something for each of us. And it was something new, unlike the things that had been passed down the chain of children.

After the gifts were open and more carols were sung, we got dressed up to go off to Christmas Day Mass at St. Matthew's—everyone but our dad, who was not Catholic. For him, this was a day of complete rest from business as usual.

After Mass and time spent trying on new clothes or playing with new toys, there was a big meal of roast beef or roast pork, potatoes, vegetables, and dessert of pie and ice cream. Inevitably Dad would say at the dinner table, "I wonder what the poor people are doing?" For a man who grew up on a farm during the Great Depression, you could not be considered poor if you had more than enough to eat.

When the meal was done and the kitchen cleaned up, we'd all pile into the station wagon and drive through the central New York snow to Uncle Floyd's farm. There, our younger uncles Jim and Jack would horse around with Betty, Dick and me, and we'd hear holiday music on the stereo by Perry Como, Johnny Mathis, Andy Williams and Nat King Cole. The latest holiday crafts made by Aunt Eula were marveled at, and we'd delight even more over her pies, cakes and cookies.

On the way home, there was more singing of the quieter Christmas tunes, while I sat on the lap of one of my older sisters, drifting in and out of sleep.

In those sweet holidays of my young childhood, I could not foresee that the peace and harmony of one future Christmas season would be threatened by a family storm.

DISCOVERING LEONA

On a rainy summer afternoon in 1963, I sat in the living room with my mother, watching TV and helping her fold laundry. My sister Betty, who had just finished her sophomore year in high school, was at the dining table in the same room, studying to get her driver's license.

I was nearing the end of fifth grade in the year that President Kennedy would be assassinated, and it was right around the time that Pope John XXIII, the great ecumenical pope, passed away. It had been about two months since my mother's mother, Grandma Catherine, had died upstairs in the bedroom that Betty and I had shared with her, until Grandma grew so ill from a series of strokes that Mom moved us to the front bedroom with our older sisters.

In the middle of an episode of the game show *Truth or Consequences*, the phone rang. The "prrring, prrring" of the heavy, black rotary phone sounded especially harsh sitting on the wood of the dining table. My sister answered it and after a few minutes said, "Mom, it's for you." As a commercial came on, Mom went to the phone and I got up to get some Kool-Aid from the kitchen. When I came back, I noticed that my mother's jaw had dropped and a disturbed look had swept over her face as she turned away from me and spoke in hushed tones.

"What's that about?" I asked Betty.

"It was the police. Something about Mom's sister," Betty answered.

"What sister? Mom doesn't have a sister," I said, aware only of Uncle Glenn and Uncle Ray as Mom's siblings.

"I don't know. Maybe they made a mistake?" she said in a curious tone.

A few minutes later my sister Diane came through the front door, home from the nearby Jesuit College where she commuted each day. By then, my mother was hanging up the phone, her eyes bleary. She said to Diane, "It's my sister Leona. They say she ran away three days ago and they just found her body by the side of the road."

The hair rose up on the back of my neck. "Ran away from what?" I probed. "I didn't know you had a sister."

"Sit down," she said to all of us. She took a tissue, dabbed her eyes and nose, and took a deep breath.

"I have an older sister, Leona. That's her name. She's been in the Willard State asylum for almost 40 years."

"Why? What was wrong with her?" I asked.

"She used to have spells. She would hear voices and see things that weren't really there," Mom said. "She got worse and worse, and one night, she came after me with a knife because the voices were telling her to kill me. That was when Grandma decided she had to go to the hospital."

The phone rang again and my mother got up quickly to answer it. It was Uncle Ray, who had also been notified by the police. At one point she raised her voice in the angry tone she used when I'd done something wrong, saying, "Why didn't they call three days ago and tell us she'd run away? And why didn't they tell us when she ran away before?"

Diane spoke quietly to Betty and me. "The picture in the front room is our Aunt Leona," she said. Since Diane was ten years older than me, I figured she had learned about Mom's sister from Grandma before she'd had all her strokes. I went to look at this image that had been to me just part of the furniture, the only nicely framed portrait in our house. It showed a gentle-looking young woman whom I had always imagined to be my mother or grandmother.

Now as I stared at it, I saw myself in her expression, her hair, and something about her eyes. I felt empathy for this unknown aunt who had run away from a lunatic asylum and may have dropped dead from exhaustion or hunger or fear. Or maybe she'd been dumped there by some crazy doctor or aide who had raped and killed her when she resisted their advances, as had happened with so many of the female Catholic saints. My chest tightened as I imagined all of the terrible possibilities.

When my mother got off the phone, she came into the front room. I yelled at her in an uncharacteristic outburst of pre-pubescent outrage, "How could you just leave your sister there all by herself for all these years and never even talk about her?" My face felt hot, my heart pounded. "You never even told me that she existed. Why didn't you visit her?"

My mother wiped her face with her apron and sat down in the large, overstuffed green-velvet chair. Even though our house was very small for ten people, we rarely sat in this front room, where our black upright piano was kept.

"We all went to visit her at first. But as the years went by, Leona didn't even know us. Before she had her strokes, Grandma and Uncle Ray would still go to see her. But I had all of you kids to care for, and it was hard to leave you to see someone who didn't even remember who I was. Grandma always said that when she died, she would come back to earth for Leona and bring her to heaven to end her suffering. I guess that's what happened."

Her words created an image in my mind of my grandmother dressed in a white gown with silver wings, like the good witch in *The Wizard of Oz*, and this calmed and soothed me. My sick aunt had been drawn away from the asylum by a grandma angel, and now they were together flying around heaven with all the saints. This helped me to forgive my mother for my harsh judgment that she had abandoned her sister.

Yet I still could not understand how or why Mom kept this family tragedy so hidden and unspoken. I was left wondering what Aunt Leona's life was like in the hospital and what drove her to chase her sister with a knife and to hear voices and see visions.

It was several days after the funeral that I overheard my mother say to one of my older sisters, "They said her thyroid was like dried shoe leather." I don't know, and probably never will know, what else Mom learned about her sister's demise. Many facts of life and death were hidden from view in our family. But it was always clear that there would be crosses to bear and that some type of suffering would always be ours as a signal that we were, indeed, people of faith.

Later that year, on September 15, 1963, a racially motivated domestic terrorist bombed the 16th Street Baptist Church in Birmingham, Alabama, and murdered four young black girls. The Church had been the site of an effort to register African-American voters. As an 11-year-old girl, the television coverage shook me with sorrow, fear and outrage.

When President Kennedy was assassinated two months later, the sisters at St. Matthew's interrupted all instruction to deliver the news that the President had been shot and killed, and they released us from school a bit early. As I walked home alone, I thought that perhaps the world was ending. Within a few days, I watched Kennedy's alleged assassin be murdered by gunfire on live television.

It was the dawn of a new era.

LEONA & WILLARD

"Man is not made better by being degraded."[3]

– Dorothea Dix

IT WAS ABOUT 30 YEARS BEFORE I was born that my maternal grandparents handed my Aunt Leona over to the care of New York State. Fortunately for Leona, by the early 20th century, New York was one of the more progressive states in caring for the mentally ill. This was owed greatly to the compassionate, pioneering efforts of the 19th-century social activist, Dorothea Dix, on behalf of those sent into government custody as "insane."[4]

During the 1840s, Dix had discovered that many Americans with cognitive or emotional disturbances were being held in county jails and poorhouses, sometimes chained and never receiving any medical treatment. Her focus on this issue in the Northeastern U.S. led to a survey in the 1860s by the New York State Surgeon General, Dr. Sylvester Willard. This survey showed that more than 1,300 people with chronic mental illness were in New York jails or almshouses, in conditions that the state's governor described as "deplorable." A resulting 1865 state law required improvements in care for the mentally ill in the state. Within a few years, an agricultural college with farmland along the shore of Seneca Lake was transformed into the Willard Asylum for the Insane, while the college moved to Ithaca where it is now known as Cornell University.

Located in Ovid Landing, the grounds are in the Finger Lakes region of New York State, an area noted today for vineyards, fresh lake recreation, expensive summer homes and beautiful, bucolic countryside. When Willard opened its doors in 1869, it featured a quality of care that was considered a major advance at that time.

But this was a low bar above which to rise, as indicated in *History of Willard Asylum for the Insane and the Willard State Hospital*, written by Robert E. Doran, M.D. in 1978. Dr. Doran had lived on the Willard grounds as a child when his father was Willard's First Assistant Physician, and he later served as the hospital's medical director. This paper, stored at the New York State Museum, is the primary source for the information about Willard in this chapter.

"For a good many years, practically all admissions came by boat," wrote Dr. Doran. "The first thing that was done was to remove their irons and chains on the dock. They were admitted, bathed, examined, dressed and fed. Kindness, gentleness and understanding were substituted for indifference, neglect, and, too often, brutality…. The form of treatment in the early days and for many years was referred to as 'moral treatment.' We would call it 'custodial care.'"[5]

Nurses, supervisors, and attendants lived on the same grounds as patients—who were called "inmates" in census records—in different rooms and buildings, but together in one shared, rural community. Inmates might be committed there for a range of reasons that made them misfits for the surrounding society. Some had physical disabilities, others had cognitive deficits and another group had physical diseases that had affected their minds. Decades prior to Willard's opening, Dorothea Dix herself had suffered physical and emotional collapse in the mid-1830s from a disease that was unknown at that time but was later identified as tuberculosis.

As with most state mental facilities around the U.S. in the 19th century, many went to Willard because they were simply unable to care for themselves: whether for physical, mental, or emotional reasons, or just because they were poor. Some were new immigrants who had trouble learning the language and ways of the new world they had entered. Only a portion had what 21st-century medicine would diagnose as a form of mental illness. Essentially, all of the inmates were there because their families—and often their doctors—didn't know what was wrong with them or how to treat or handle them. In some cases, their families had abandoned them or were thousands of miles away in another state or country. Whatever the underlying cause of their ailment, they were labeled "insane" and housed in a large state institution.

By the late 1880s, the Willard Asylum was advertised as a tourist attraction. According to Doran, boatloads of sightseers arrived "to have picnics on the grounds and be amused by the patients." Within ten years, the disruption of this "tourism" and theft by visitors from Willard's gardens led to the installation of a barbed-wire fence, not to keep the inmates in, but to keep the "sane" sightseers out.

Originally established for chronic cases of mental illness from all over New York State, by 1890, Willard accepted an increasing number of acute and chronic cases from the surrounding region. In the early 1920s, when my Aunt Leona began suffering from increasingly disturbing hallucinations as a young adult, state mental institutions became her home. As with many other patients at such facilities during the late 19th and early 20th century, Aunt Leona contracted tuberculosis (TB) after her initial hospitalization at an asylum in Utica, New York. Since Willard had built a TB pavilion for women in 1908, she was probably transferred there for specialized care at some point in the 1920s. She would remain at Willard for the rest of her life.

My mother told my older siblings that Leona had suffered from a very large goiter on her thyroid gland. While this can be easily treated today, and may have been understood by some American doctors by the 1920s, it was a medical mystery in central New York at that time. Aunt Leona's thyroid illness was a likely cause of her hallucinations and "spells," but no doctor who cared for her then knew how to diagnose it, let alone how to treat it. Along with many others suffering from physical ailments, such as syphilis that would one day be treatable, her parents and doctors designated Leona as "insane" and committed her to an asylum.

For most of Willard's existence, patients there were encouraged but not required to work. Records from the 1880s indicate that about 40 percent of the patients engaged in work activities, including farming and gardening, grounds maintenance, laundry, kitchen work, carpentry, painting, cobbling, tailoring and sewing. Doran quotes Dr. John B. Chapin, Willard Medical Superintendent from 1869 to 1884, "…the diversion of a large proportion of the insane from the mental state in which they are incapacitated for self-support or self-preservation to their own ordinary avocations is a result to be desired second only to recovery. The habits, sleep and physical condition are improved. Life is rendered more tolerable. Mental quietude is promoted, and paroxysmal excitement is lessened."[6]

Because even direct descendants of mental institution patients in New York State are not allowed access to the records of the "inmates," my siblings and I—who are my Aunt Leona's only remaining living relatives—will never know whether our aunt was able to assume any work assignments at Willard. But we know that she did needlework at home before she was sent away, so we can imagine her on a team of women who may have used colorful threadwork to decorate the inmate clothing, pillows and curtains that were made by inmate-patients at Willard. This speculation is comforting, because it means our aunt may have found some pleasure in an activity and a feeling of accomplishment by contributing to her asylum community.

Aunt Leona entered Willard during or just after the First World War, a period when the asylum suffered from a shortage of help. By 1924, New York's governor, Alfred Smith, turned the state's attention once again to improvements in care within state institutions for the mentally ill and disabled, and numerous improvements were made to the Willard facilities. In the 1930s, federal law established eight-hour days for ward employees, and a 42-hour course of instruction for attendants helped to set and maintain standards for care.

But the Second World War took its toll on those employees who remained at Willard. According to Doran, "In 1943, there were 95 male ward employees trying to perform the duties of 217."[7] The state legislature increased salaries to encourage workers to stay, and provided overtime pay and commuting expenses for those who lived off the grounds. After 1945, student nurses working at Willard were able to receive training in psychiatry, in-service programs and refresher courses.

Despite the increase in care, tuberculosis was a leading cause of death at Willard and many other state institutions for decades, until antibiotics were discovered and mass-produced during and after World War II. Other leading causes of mortality at Willard in the late 19th and early 20th century included syphilis and pneumonia; rampant illnesses included diphtheria and typhoid fever. Willard was hit hard by the global influenza epidemic of 1918 and 1919, with 486 patients stricken and 90 deaths. In addition to patient illness, nearly 200 officers and employees fell ill with that flu, and two died.

We know from Doran's history that after 1885, Willard always had a woman physician available for gynecological exams. She lived onsite along with junior physicians and interns. Again, it is some consolation to know that our Aunt Leona may have had a woman doctor for that type of medical care.

Willard's medical directors tried a range of therapies for mental illness over the decades. When Elliott Hall was built on the grounds in 1931, elaborate hydrotherapy equipment was installed, but it was not proven to work. By 1937, insulin shock treatment and Metrazol[8] were in use, and electroshock was substituted within a few years. Less invasive treatments included occupational therapies and recreational therapies, such as music. Without access to her medical records, our family has no idea whether Aunt Leona received any of these treatments.

By 1955, Willard was like most other state mental institutions in using psychotropic drugs to tranquilize patients. To describe treatment in the 1960s, Doran quotes from Willard State Hospital's annual report ending in March 31, 1965:

> Both individual and group psychotherapy are used extensively. The modern psychiatric drugs, both tranquilizers and anti-depressants, are frequently used and Anectine modified electroshock therapy is also given. There has been much expansion in activities during the year in an-

cillary programs including occupational therapy, recreational therapy, voluntary activities, religious programs, social service and psychological functions which are carried out in all major hospital services.[9]

For most of its history, Willard State Hospital was a heavily self-reliant and ecologically contained community. Doran has documented that its farmland yielded large quantities of various goods, including wheat, corn, alfalfa and oats, vegetables, fruits, such as apples, grapes and berries, and livestock for milk, eggs and meat. The bakery made enriched bread using soy flour and vitamins that bore the name Willard Bread while its shops produced clothing, shoes, towels, sheets and mattresses; its yards and quarries yielded bricks, lime and stone. Its fallen timber was used for repairs, construction, bushel crates, and sawdust for icehouses and pigpens. Baskets, chairs and floor polishers were made in the broom shop; pots, pans, basins and more were made in the tin shop. In the days before electrical refrigeration, ice came from the upper reservoir and pond for icehouse storage. The dairy herd produced between eight and ten thousand pounds of milk per cow in the 1920s and '30s.

According to Doran, "The farm and garden always made a profit.... As most of the work was done by the patients, good supervision was necessary."[10]

Doran reports that many were saddened by the governor's decision in 1960 to close down the farm at Willard. Furthermore, the quieting impact of drugs on those hospitalized for mental illness had become a tool for intensive political efforts to reduce the patient population. In the 1960s, Willard became the first hospital in New York State to have a full-time Rehabilitation Service, with physical, social and vocational services, some located inside the hospital but many increasingly located in the community. Between 1962 and 1977, the census at Willard State Hospital dropped from 2,582 to 890.

In 1963, after the farm at Willard had closed and drugs were widely used to control patients, my Aunt Leona escaped from the institution for the second time within just a few weeks. My siblings and I have no further details about how this happened. Not until three days after the second escape did the authorities notify our mother and uncle that Leona had died by the side of the road from exposure.

Under New York State law, because Leona had no direct descendants, we have to wait until several months after the 50th anniversary of her death to obtain her death certificate, despite the fact that we are her only living relatives. In late 2013, my siblings and I hope to learn whether a medical examiner had ever confirmed the cause of her death, a mystery we have hoped to solve for decades.

In 1995, Willard closed its doors for good. Today, the New York State Museum houses a collection of suitcases and personal effects taken from patients upon their arrival at the asylum, and several web sites host online historic and recent photographs of Willard's buildings and grounds.[11]

THE FARM

BORN IN THE GERMAN WINE REGION of Baden, my paternal grandfather, Frederick Carl Wagner, moved with his parents to the U.S. in 1882 when he was five years old. His father had farmed near the small German town of Lipburg, but in Syracuse, New York, he became a brewer. Both of Frederick's parents succumbed to tuberculosis before they reached the age of 40, and so Grandpa Frederick—adopted by a relative at age 13—went to work rather than complete his education.

By 1910, Frederick was 33 years old, married with a newborn daughter. With years of experience on a neighbor's farm, he purchased his own 52-acre farm on Freemont Road in East Syracuse in central New York where apple trees had grown for many decades. Frederick made farming his sole employment, raising apples and other fruits, along with grains, vegetables, dairy cows, chickens and pigs. By 1921, Frederick's wife Lena had borne three more children. The youngest, Mari Louise, was just a few weeks old when Lena died from complications after childbirth, leaving Frederick Carl as a single father of four. Eveleen was the eldest at only ten years old, while my father, Frederick Ernest, was seven; his younger brother Floyd was four.

The senior Frederick gave up the newborn for adoption by another family in the area and hired a housekeeper to tend to his home and older children. Since farming alone could not support the family, he began a second job as a machinist with the New York Central Railroad. In the late 19th century, this rail line connected freight from Midwestern farms and factories with steamboats on the Hudson River, giving upstate New York farmers new competition for the growing market of downstate New York City consumers.

Many changes arrived on the farm after World War II ended. Well water for drinking was replaced by the village supply piped from Lake Ontario, and an outhouse was replaced by indoor plumbing. By 1947 at age 69, Frederick Carl had grown ill and was lame with arthritis. Though he still worked on the farm when he could, he sold his interest in the property that year to my Uncle Floyd. In 1953, Frederick Carl died of stomach cancer at the age of 75, a lifespan about twice as long as that of his parents.

Floyd worked literally around the clock—in the fields from 7 AM until sundown, and then, after supper and a nap, on the night shift at the railroad in the 1940s or later at the General Motors plant. Floyd and a handful of family members handled all labor on his 52-acre farm. In their hours after housework, school or jobs, Floyd's wife, daughter, sister Eveleen and two half-brothers Jack and Jim—born after his father Frederick Carl had remarried in 1930—all lent their hands in the fields and orchards. He sold his apples directly to farm visitors, farm stands, and in the 1960s and 1970s to his brother Fred's–my father's–Mohegan Market grocery store in nearby Rome.

In the early morning every autumn when I was a child, the Fred Wagner family would pile into the car to get apples from the farm. While my mother would request Northern Spy apples for baking, our favorite eating apple was a Macintosh apple–

more crisp, flavorful and juicy than any apple I've ever eaten since. We'd have fresh apple cider and fresh-baked apple pie made by Aunt Eula.

Throughout the 1950s, the Wagner farm had grain crops and livestock. But sometime around 1960, Uncle Floyd took the incentive offered by the federal government to put the grain fields into the "soil bank." The newfound time and money was invested in developing the apple orchards, and in other fruits such as peaches, pears, plums, prunes and grapes. He did some breeding and grafting to improve the apples and the yield. He was very selective about the apples sold as his "firsts," or "seconds," and any sign of rot kept blemished apples out of the cider mill.

In addition to hard work, the farm "was the place for family members to gather for the holidays and other family get-togethers. It was always a time of great food and sharing of family fun," said Floyd in conversations with his brother Jim in 1997. The games included cards played with family and friends, ping pong in the kitchen, and croquet on the lawn outside the farm home.

After Floyd's first wife of 50 years died, he decided to sell the farm. Unfortunately, no one in the family was in a position to take it on and in 1990, land that had been in the Wagner family for more than 80 years passed out of the family's hands. The new owner made more than a million dollars by harvesting topsoil behind the barn and selling it to a nearby town for a landfill. He later sold the property to a young couple who are committed to keeping the farm intact and maintaining some of the orchards for their family's use. Floyd died in 2007, and the rest of the orchards are now growing wild.[12]

LOST SISTERS SHARED

THE PORTS WERE A HARD-WORKING, GOD-FEARING American family. Catherine, whose maiden name was Kalin, and her husband, Franklin Port, were church-going Catholics. By 1923, Catherine was 44, and Franklin, a railroad man, was about 12 years her senior. Their older son Ray was in engineering school while Eleanor, my mother, was a sensitive and reserved 10-year-old who excelled in her school studies. Their younger son Glenn was eight years older than Eleanor, and would have been about 16 when his eldest sibling, Leona, went completely mad at 21.

Grandma Catherine Port left no written family record that tells us when Leona began having her spells, but it was around 1923 when she was committed to the asylum. My sisters Joan and Diane remember our mother saying that Leona knew when a spell was coming. She would neatly put away her needlepoint and await the storm that was about to explode in her brain.

Grandma Catherine spent a great deal of time outdoors in the summer, grooming a garden full of hydrangea, poppies, nasturtium, irises and more. Alongside and behind the flower garden were fruit trees, raspberry bushes and a grape arbor. Decades after Catherine began these gardens and after arthritis and strokes kept her from them, they still bore fruit and flowers galore in the summer. As her youngest grandchild, I had the pleasure of playing there, enjoying their beauty, and eating their grapes, berries, cherries and pears.

My mother always bemoaned her belief that she did not inherit Grandma's green thumb, but I suspect that she simply devoted her time and energy to different pursuits. Like Leona, when she was not doing schoolwork, Eleanor focused on the feminine textile crafts of needlepoint, sewing, embroidery, knitting and mending the household's clothing. Later in life, she often said that she had dreamed of being a medical laboratory scientist, a goal that seemed impossible to young girls who were afraid to defy convention in that era.

My mother had the greatest admiration for her older brother Ray, who became a successful electrical engineer, with a lovely home in Brewerton, north of East Syracuse, along the banks of Oneida Lake. And yet there was sorrow within this success, as Ray's wife Ethel had a multitude of miscarriages that kept their marriage barren.

As Glenn grew older, he followed in his dad's footsteps and worked on the railroad. He traveled with the train and somewhere along the way, he developed some bad habits. He chewed tobacco and spit out the juice, drank far too much and had women friends in various way stations. My older sisters say he never really outgrew being a mama's boy, even though he met a woman later in his life that straightened him out and helped him get off the bottle and onto the wagon. But like Ray, he never had children, and as far as we know, neither did his sister Leona.

And so, Eleanor was the only one of Catherine's children who would have children of her own. And since Catherine was the only one in her generation to have her own children, we six Port/Wagner kids were the only children to carry on the

Kalen/Port genes from Grandma Catherine or her husband, Grandpa Frank Port.

With a smidgen of understanding about genetics in the 1940s and 1950s, my mother knew that if a gene for madness had sent Leona to the asylum, it could surface again in one of her children.

It's difficult to talk about the Port family of East Syracuse without mentioning the Great Depression. They didn't have much to begin with, so they didn't have a lot to lose when the stock market crashed in 1929. But their lives, from 1929 to the late 1940s, were shaped by shortages and constraints on opportunity. It's likely that my parents' very marriage was built on the limits faced by young adults of their day.

As a young teenager, I asked Mom why she decided to marry my father the year both of them turned 25. She said, "He was the only one who was still coming around."

By 1938, Fred—who had dropped out of engineering school at Syracuse University—had a job at a local grocery store. He gave Eleanor a ring and they were married in November that year. Since my mother was Catholic and my father Protestant, the priest would not allow them to have a church wedding. With only their friends Dot and George as witnesses, the wedding took place in the rectory of St. Matthew's Church.

My parents had very different personalities, but one thing they had in common was the loss of close family members during the 1920s. My dad had lost his mother, Lena, and his new baby sister, Mari Louise, in 1920 when he was just seven years old. The farm family that adopted the baby lived nearby, but they were more affluent than the Wagners. Perhaps because her new parents did not want this child to know that she was adopted, there was virtually no interaction between her and her siblings.

For decades, well into his adulthood, my father harbored negative feelings toward this younger sister. It may have been due to jealousy at her better fortune, or because of an unchecked childhood belief that she was to blame for the death of his mother.

Late in his life, my dad told me that his father fell into a deep depression after his wife Lena's death. He also told me that, not long before she died, one of his uncles had taken a shotgun into the field near the farm and shot himself to death. When he told me this story, he sat in his usual seat at the dining room table, a cigarette between his fingers, smoke curling in the air as a fearful look spread across his face and tears welled up in his eyes.

"Dad was so sad after my mother died, I was afraid he would do what Uncle Gene did. That he might," he hesitated a long moment before continuing, "...that he might take his own life."

As with the tale of his little sister, Dad had hidden this story from me until I had children of my own. While I had known at a younger age that his mother had died after childbirth, I had never thought about what had happened to the baby that was born. Like Mom's sister Leona, this aunt was a mystery—another close relative whom I never had the opportunity to meet or know. I now know that her name was Mari Louise, and I've seen photos of her and met her sons, my first cousins, in recent years at extended family reunions.

But as a child, I was influenced by a shared, underlying and unexplained sense of shame surrounding these lost sisters that pervaded our home.

UNEARTHING ANTONIO A. SAINZ DE LA PINA

WHILE MY PARENTS ENDURED THE SHORTAGES of World War II and raised their first three little girls, a contemporary named Anthony Sainz (Antonio A. Sainz de la Pina) worked for the Batista regime in Cuba. At that point, Fred and Eleanor Wagner did not know that Anthony Sainz existed, let alone that they would pay him medical fees nearly 30 years later to treat their youngest daughter, who was not yet born.

Born in Havana of parents who moved to New York City when he was a young child, Anthony A. Sainz had returned to his parents' homeland during the 1930s to attend college and medical school. According to newspaper accounts from the 1950s that were probably derived from biographical information provided directly by Sainz, he reportedly earned numerous degrees in Cuba, including an A.B., B. Sc., Ph.D., and M.D.[13] In 1941, he completed his medical degree at the University of Havana Medical School, and soon thereafter, he conducted research for the Ministry of Public Health, the Finlay Institute for Research of Havana, and the University Medical School.[14]

The name Sainz or Saenz was originally associated with Sephardic Jews who settled in Spain and Portugal, many of whom left Europe or converted to Catholicism during the Inquisition. If he was Jewish by ancestry, it would be understandable if Anthony Sainz had a particular interest in witnessing the end of the Nazi regime, after it had slaughtered millions of European Jews. When World War II ended with Germany and Japan's surrender, there were new opportunities overseas. Possibly recruited by Dr. Herbert Abrams, who traveled to Cuban to recruit doctors for the post-war recovery effort,[15] Dr. Sainz became one of the medical directors for the United Nations Relief and Rehabilitation Administration (UNRRA) in the U.S. Zone of Occupation in Germany.

The United Nations Relief and Rehabilitation Administration (UNRRA) was an international relief agency, largely dominated by the United States but representing 44 nations. Founded in 1943, it became part of the United Nations in 1945, was especially active in 1945 and 1946, and largely shut down operations in 1947. Its purpose was to "plan, co-ordinate, administer or arrange for the administration of measures for the relief of victims of war in any area under the control of any of the United Nations through the provision of food, fuel, clothing, shelter and other basic necessities, medical and other essential services." Its worldwide staff of nearly 25,000 was funded by many nations, and totaled nearly four billion dollars.[16]

During the 1950s, American newspapers reported that Sainz served "with the Cuban Navy with the rank of Commander until 1942," and that "as a civilian he was associate professor of general pathology at Havana University and technical advisor to the Cuban Ministry of Public Health."[17] There are some news accounts that also cite Sainz's accomplishments between 1945 and 1947 as earning him a citation from the Third Army, the French Legion, and the Cuban Order of Finlay.[18] At the end of this assignment, Sainz returned to the nation where he had grown up, the U.S.A., where he went to work as a Research Fellow at Cornell

University and at Charles B. Towne Hospital in New York. In 1950, he moved to Iowa to work at the Mental Health Institute in Cherokee, Iowa. According to the Institute's records provided by its library archivist, Sainz was there from September 18, 1950 to October 9, 1954 as a "resident psychiatrist," until he left to continue his training in Iowa City.[19]

Newspaper accounts regarding Anthony Sainz from the 1950s and later investigations tell some more colorful stories about his titles, responsibilities, and activities in Iowa. It was midway through Sainz's tenure at the Mental Health Institute in Cherokee, Iowa, that I was born in Syracuse, New York.

Leona Port – close-up from a
school class photograph

Aunt Leona – portrait that
hung in the front room of
the Port-Wagner home in
East Syracuse

Leona with brothers Glenn and Ray

Leona, not long before she was committed, with her little sister Eleanor and their Aunt Fannie

The Port family after Leona was committed – At top: Grandma Catherine (Kalin) Port, 2nd row: Grandpa Franklin Port (with pipe), unidentified, 3rd row: unidentified woman friend, Glenn Port, bottom: Eleanor Port (Wagner), Ray Port

Patients farming at Willard State Hospital

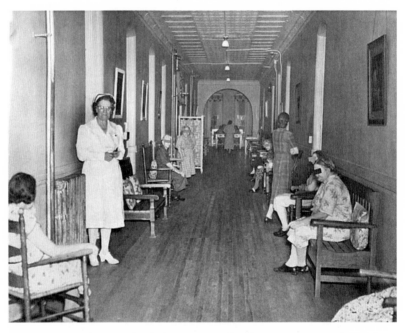

Patients and staff inside Willard State Hospital

All images of Willard State Hospital courtesy of Roger Luther,
www.nysAsylum.com

Winter View of Chapin House, Willard State Hospital. Willard, N. Y.

Linda's great-grandfather Frederick Carl Wagner (top right) and his family. Linda's paternal grandfather Frederick is at the lower left.

The Wagner Farm home
On the Wagner family farm in central New York State, a broad range of
crops were grown until the federal government began to provide "soil
bank" subsidies to farmers in the 1950s.

Wagner Farm – aerial view, 1953. Farm photos courtesy of
James R. Wagner, Wagner & Allied Families Scrapbook.

Grandpa Frederick Wagner before his death in 1953 (lower left) at the family farm with daughter Eveleen (seated) and (back row) sons Frederick Ernest and Floyd (of first wife Lena) and sons James and John (of second wife Anna).

My father's baby sister, Marilouise (Wagner), shown here at age 15, was adopted by the Carhart family after her birth mother Lena died.

Marilouise married Arthur Bohus and they had two sons. She's shown here at her 70th birthday party.

III

TRANSITIONS:
THE CONTEXT OF MEMORY

GOOD FRIDAY

INSIDE ST. MATTHEW'S CHURCH AT 2 pm on Good Friday in 1964, the lights were dim. I had been silent for two hours at that point and had already completed one round of the Stations of the Cross. The carved statues depicting Christ's tribulations, recessed in the walls on the sides of the main part of the church, were all visible. But all other statues—of the Blessed Virgin, the Sacred Heart, Joseph, and the many other saints—were covered in the deep purple drapes of Lent, when we were bound as good Catholics to sacrifice joy and pleasure in anticipation of the death of Christ.

I was what kids in the sixth grade "B" class would have called a "goody two shoes" and kids of the late 20th century would have called a religious "nerd"—a devout child who spoke up to her peers to chastise their laughter and fooling around during Mass. This outraged me most at the moment of transubstantiation—that time when the altar boys rang the bells and the priest raised the round, white, flat bread-like host up high toward the ceiling, and then followed with the chalice filled with wine—to mark the transformation of bread and wine into the body and blood of Jesus.

I had accurately memorized the catechism to ensure I was ready for First Communion in first grade. And in sixth grade, I had correctly answered all questions required for Confirmation by the Bishop.

On this Good Friday, I poured my entire body, mind and soul into the suffering of Christ. I imagined in gory detail the terrible betrayal by a disciple he had trusted; even though in his omnipotence, he knew in advance that the trust would not be warranted. My mind evoked as vividly as possible what it felt like to have thick sharp thorns pounded into and through your skull, as the Roman soldiers had done to the Lord while laughing at his misery.

Meditating on the mockery by all those who had stood along the path Jesus walked toward the hill at Calvary, I did my best to feel the pain of having my hands and feet nailed to a wooden cross while its splinters pierced the skin on my back. I recalled what it feels like when your lips are cracked and you get some vinegar into the split skin if you're eating salad dressing, because the soldiers purposely gave Him vinegar instead of water when he said he was thirsty.

Now I was at the point where Our Lord was just hanging on the cross, waiting to die for all the sins that my fellow human beings and I had ever committed throughout history. I prayed for forgiveness for myself and everyone in the world. I contemplated suffering, death, grief and that brief moment of doubt when Jesus cried out, "Eloi, eloi, lama sabachthani?" (My God, My God, why have you forsaken me?)

At the age of 11 and-a-half, I could relate personally to all of Christ's suffering. I had embraced the Catholic blues.

* * *

The seeds of doubt sprout when you least expect them.

Just outside of East Syracuse, down Erie Boulevard, was Robert Hall, a small box-shaped clothing store frequented by working families for back-to-school shopping. By the late summer of 1964, I had shot up after years of being one of the three shortest and skinniest kids in my class. It was rare in those years that I would get new clothes. As the youngest of six, I usually sported well-worn hand-me-downs from my four older sisters, and on rare occasions, even from my brother.

Since St. Matthew's Parochial School required girls to wear a plain forest-green jumper with St. Matt's insignia over the heart, I didn't need many new clothes for school. The only things on my list were a couple of new, white, regulation-style blouses with a Peter-Pan collar, a couple of tank-top undershirts, socks and shoes. So on this day, Mom drove to Robert Hall with me in the front seat and my brother Dick in the back.

I asked for penny loafers, so popular with my college-aged sisters, and I had hidden in my clothes drawer two shiny new pennies for the shoe slots. Robert Hall didn't have my size in the penny loafers, but that didn't deter my mother.

"They have a pair a half-size up from your size, Lin. Let's try these." Mom never called me Linda, only Lin, or "young lady" if I was in trouble. She had planned to name me Lynne Marie, she once told me, but she allowed my older siblings to vote on the choices, and Linda Mary won out instead.

"Mom, these fall off my heel when I walk and they don't feel good."

"We can put tissues in the toes. You're growing so fast; these will fit you in no time."

There was no further discussion as she put the shoes in the box and took all the goods to the checkout. I didn't really mind the loose shoes that much since I was getting something new. Besides, I was getting a chance to spend some rare time with my mother. Now that the three oldest were in college and Dick usually worked after school, Mom had a little more time and money for Betty and me.

It was close to dinnertime and Mom was in a hurry to get home and prepare the meal with my grandmother. The door on the passenger side of our aqua-colored station wagon had been stuck closed for weeks. So I climbed into the car from my mother's side and crawled over to the passenger side as Dick climbed into the back. I was chattering away, enjoying my time with Mom, thrilled to have new clothes and shoes and excited about the prospect of starting fifth grade, which meant moving up to the second floor of our Catholic elementary school.

The only time I had been on the second floor of the school was when my fourth-grade teacher, Sister Mary John, had been so impressed by my reading ability that she made me read an entire 4th grader's book to the giant 8th graders while standing on an enormous chair in front of the entire classroom. As I described this scene to my mother, telling her how severe my stage fright had been, I leaned against the passenger side door.

Usually, Mom would have slowed down for the yellow stop light in front of us, but in her haste to get home to dinner, she stepped on the gas to make the left turn off the boulevard onto the road toward the bridge back home. Just after she had rounded the center of the intersection, the door popped open and I slid out of the car onto the road, screaming all the way.

My arms were straight out in front of me, and I felt like a bird that had flown a little too close to the ground while swooping down from the sky to catch a worm. My forearms hit first and since my eyes were wide open, I could see specks of tiny gray stones rising up in a fine mist of dust around me. Next, my chest and then my legs followed, skidding along the pavement in the kind of slow motion shown on TV when there's a judgment call needed to determine whether the base runner who just slid into second should be called "safe" or "out." At this moment, there was only me and the surface of the road. I gave no thought to the cars that nearly hit me or my mother and brother, who could not see where or how I had landed.

And like a baseball player sliding into base, I jumped back up just as quickly as I hit the ground. I hopped back into our car pulled over to the side, my heart pounding and longing for a joyous, welcoming embrace back to the world of soft, warm human contact.

"Oh my God, are you OK?" my mother asked. Without reaching out to hug or kiss me, she gave me an anxious visual exam. Dick tried to make light of the situation, but he had a worried, even guilty, look on his face. The door had been stuck because he had a scrape while driving the car a few weeks before.

"Yeah, I'm OK, I'm all right," but I still didn't feel quite right and I was not sure why. I examined my arms—luckily, I had been wearing long sleeves since it was a cool day for late summer. The sleeves on both arms were torn, and my arms were scraped and had little stones embedded in the skin. The pants I was wearing had protected my legs pretty well, though there were also holes in the knees and brush burns on my legs.

Some vague unease was not erased when we arrived home and my mother cleaned up my skinned arms and legs with the skill of a nurse in a clinic. The unease remained when my father came home and I ran to greet him to tell him I almost got killed today, and he knelt down and gave me a big bear hug. The discomfort was still there when Mom told my father, "I was never so glad to see someone get up so fast."

Old enough to know intellectually that this accident was not my mother's fault, I still felt a desire to blame her. It was many years later that I came to understand that my desire was not about falling out of the car, but about something that was missing when I popped up and got back into the car. Without the benefit of a big bear hug, a kiss and maybe some tears, without her deep concern and affection physically displayed, I began to lose trust that my mother had the capability to shield me from harm.

DAD'S STORY

Having lost his own mother when he was only seven and she just 35, my father appreciated the maternal presence of his mother-in-law. He called her "Mother" affectionately until she passed away after a series of strokes in January 1963. But for decades, it had gnawed at his self-esteem that he could not earn enough in the early years of his marriage to afford a home for his wife and six children. Instead, he and his nuclear family shared the small, tar-and-speckle shingled house with Grandma Catherine and her son Glenn, who was eight years older than Fred and his wife Eleanor, but much younger in emotional maturity.

In addition to Dad's nagging sense of failure that the house represented, the type of fun that helped him relax and enjoy himself could not be nurtured in a three-bedroom, one-bath house stuffed with four adults and six children. So, when it was payday, he did what so many other men in the sorry village of East Syracuse did. He cashed the paycheck and spent the first dollars at a bar. In Dad's case, the bar was at the American Legion hall on Main Street, where you could shoot pool, down a few beers with whisky chasers for a few bucks, and leer at and flirt with the women who went there craving any type of male attention.

While it may have seemed to my mother that her husband was wasting his hard-earned pay, which was so badly needed for clothing, household items and repairs at home, Fred felt that his success in the grocery business ensured that his family was always well-fed. And unlike many husbands and fathers who drank on payday, he never raised a hand against his wife or children. Generally, his drinking was a safety valve that left him jolly from a little playtime after a hard six-day workweek.

But more important to the entire family, Dad's work-hard, play-hard sensibility, combined with a keen head for math, an eye for tasteful detail and a dedication to customer service made my father an excellent manager, marketer and small businessman at a time of opportunity in America.

Having started in the grocery business as a bag boy during the Great Depression, he learned the butcher trade and gradually worked his way up to a position as general manager of the entire northeast regional chain of Mohican Markets. Named after a Native American tribe of the Hudson River in New York State, Mohican Markets had a headdress as its logo in those years. Mohawk Valley historian Bob Cudmore describes the rich sensory memories that patrons of Mohican Markets recall in a June 2009 column titled "Life in 1946" and published in the *Daily Gazette* of Schenectady, New York.

> There once were Mohican Markets in many of the formerly bustling downtowns of the Northeast. There were Mohican Markets in the cities of Massachusetts, Connecticut and in Troy, Syracuse, Niagara Falls, Binghamton and elsewhere in New York. Emil Suda of Amsterdam recalled that you used to get a whiff of fish walking into the Mohican, 'As a young boy, one of the oddities remembered about the market was the place-

ment of wooden barrels of fresh fish out on the sidewalk, near the entrance door at any time of the year.' In particular, Suda remembered the salt smell of baccala or codfish in brine.

If you got past the fish, the fragrance of the bakery was next. Suda said the Mohican had a fine bakery department with store-baked cakes, pies and other pastries displayed in glass cases. The floor was sprinkled with green sawdust. In January 1946, the Mohican advertised two lobsters for $1.25. A chocolate or coconut layer cake could be yours for 50 cents. Mince pies were 35 cents each.[20]

After he became a general manager, Dad was often on the road six days out of the week and rarely came home before 8 pm, long after his mother-in-law, wife and the children had eaten dinner. When he finally arrived at home, we were expected to be quiet.

Nevertheless, my father and I had an evening ritual. When he first came in the door, I ran to him and he picked me up. Decades later, he would chuckle to recall how I always patted him on the back as he held me. After eating his dinner, he sat in his favorite stuffed chair in the living room. It was my job to sit on the chair behind him and comb his hair from the nape of his neck up. He would take off his glasses, close his eyes and smile. The big brown mole on his forehead that distinguished him without looking unattractive always fascinated me.

Sunday was usually a day for Dad to relax at home, play golf with his childhood buddies, or pile the whole family into the station wagon for a picnic at the lake or a trip to his brother's farm.

I remember only one time when Dad was at home taking care of me while Mom and Grandma were away. I was playing in the kitchen and smacked my head on the corner of a cupboard. Unlike Mom, he did not just give me a bag of ice to put on my own head; he picked me up, sat me on his lap and held the ice on my forehead himself. In retrospect, whatever his failings, the limited sense I had for physical affection came from my father, not my mother.

Move to Rome

EVENTUALLY THE SERVICE GROCERY BUSINESS, WITH on-site bakeries and butcher shops, gave way to supermarket chains and foods that were processed and packaged hundreds and thousands of miles away. As this transition began to take root, my dad had an opportunity to purchase one of the best positioned Mohican stores, 50 miles away from our hometown, and he seized the chance. At age 49, with only $5,000 in the bank and no other financial cushion, he bought the Rome, NY store, which he later renamed "Mohegan Market." The Mohegan are another Native American tribe, originally living in what we now know as Connecticut.

The employees at the Rome store already knew Fred since the store was on his General Manager rounds. An inch shy of six feet, Fred was a tall man for his generation and the demographics of his upstate NY locale. With thinning brown hair and glasses, his distinctive forehead mole, lively long gait, broad smile and friendly demeanor, he radiated warmth and engendered loyalty among staff and customers.

By 1964, my father had been running his own store for nearly two years. Both my Grandma Catherine and Uncle Glenn had passed away, Catherine from complications of strokes and Glenn from liver disease. Despite early signs of political upheaval, the U.S. economy was strong, and business was excellent at the Mohegan Market in Rome. Of the six children, only two remained at home—me, about to finish 6th grade, and my sister Betty, who was not happy about attending St. John the Evangelist High School in downtown Syracuse.

My parents decided, after 26 years of marriage and more than 50 years—their entire lifetimes—of living in East Syracuse, to move their remaining family to Rome, NY. The home of Griffiss Air Force base, Rome Cable, and Revere Copper and Brass would now be where we called home.

Betty and I joined my mother in the search for a new house, a novelty that amazed, excited and inspired us, but at the same time filled us with low-grade anxiety and trepidation. The idea of leaving friends, relatives and familiar places to enter a new world of people, sights, smells and sounds was nerve wracking.

We were moving from a cramped 100-year-old house whose stone basement still featured a coal cellar and a furnace that my mother beat with a rubber hose to ensure that it would start up on cold winter nights. The new house, built just a few years before we moved, came complete with a dishwasher, a bar in the basement and our very own bedrooms. This was utter luxury we had never imagined, and it seemed that our parents had struck it rich. Instead of policemen, mechanics and disabled elderly as neighbors, we would live next door to a doctor and across from a pharmacist. Stately hedges surrounded our neatly trimmed property, and there were no forts in the woods or hiding spots in high grass—just playhouses in backyards on well-groomed carpets of evenly-cut green lawn.

I went with my mother while she shopped for all new furniture and drapes. The sofa she selected was slightly curved and covered with fine turquoise upholstery with a soft sheen, and she chose a matching easy chair and recliner. The draperies were cream colored with a touch of turquoise thread woven into the regal-looking raised pattern. My older sisters were in awe of the selections she made, never realizing that my mother had some aesthetic taste of her own that she never before had the chance to express. To the elder siblings, Betty and I were being spoiled. Things came too easy to us, and we didn't know the true value of money and hard work, they said.

But our father felt that he was finally able to provide for his family in a manner that satisfied him. Not only was there always high-quality fresh food on the table, but also the table, dining room, and kitchen were all new. At long last, his wife had some dignity, and he could give her an occasional break from housework by taking her out for Sunday dinner.

His two youngest children who remained at home had just a short distance to the bus or an easy walk to Catholic schools. And his son Richard had accepted his offer to work with him at the store, so it seemed that he had an heir apparent to the family business.

For the first time, Fred was the king of his castle, and since he had also become his own boss, he began to see himself as, and behave as, a benevolent dictator.

THE CONTEXT OF PLACE: ROME, NEW YORK

THE CITY OF ROME IS NESTLED in rolling hills and valleys along the Mohawk River in central New York State. The 2011 website for the city of Rome offered this information about the city's history:

> Historical Rome, NY, incorporated in 1870, is a city of 72 square miles conveniently located in the geographical center of NYS at the foothills of the Adirondacks.[21] Due to its strategic location, it was considered one of the most important transportation points for people and goods along the great passage during the settling and founding of our nation in the 1700-1800's. In 1758, Fort Stanwix was constructed to protect the great Carrying Place and its settlers. The first shovel of dirt was turned at Rome for the Erie Canal which bridged the gap between waterways to enable travel and opened the American West. During the Industrial Revolution, Rome gained the reputation as the "Copper City" as its metal industries produced an estimated 10% of all copper in the US. Throughout the centuries, our great city has been home to many of our country's pioneering minds and remarkable patriots.[22]

By the end of the 20th century, Rome—like so many other former industrial American cities—was just a shell of its former self. As U.S. businesses gradually shifted their manufacturing plants to places where unions and regulation held less sway, companies fled upstate New York. After the U.S. involvement in Vietnam came to a whimpering end, Griffiss Air Force Base was gradually shut down. Rome, like its European namesake, could be a symbol for the end of an empire. When we lived there, its decline was just beginning.

As might be expected in a city named Rome, more than 20% of the residents have Italian ancestry. One of the city's major events was the festival at the Italian Catholic Church, St. John the Baptist, where the tempting scent of pizza frite—fried pizza dough covered in powdered sugar—filled the air and the sound of bocce balls knocking into each other was punctuated by shouts of "Vincere!"

Other ethnic ancestries included German, Irish and Polish, and each established its own Roman Catholic Church in town—St. Mary's for the Germans, Transfiguration for the Polish, and St. Peter's for the Irish. There were other Christian denominations in Rome, and a few Jewish families, but the Roman Catholics had enough children to fill a 500-student high school in the 1960s.

As a teenager in Rome, you often learned where your friend's parents worked. Rome was best known during that period as the home of Griffiss Air Force Base, built during World War II. During the Vietnam War, the base was the headquarters for air defense command in the northeastern U.S. The 416th Bombardment Wing based at Griffiss supported B-52 missions in Southeast Asia. Many civilians who lived in Rome during this period worked on the base, and for years it was the largest employer in Oneida County. The military was so central to Rome's identity that there is an online museum devoted to the connection.[23]

Other major employers in and near Rome included manufacturers such as Revere Copper & Brass, whose origins included a Massachusetts firm founded in 1801 by none other than Paul Revere. In addition to the manufacture of a range of copper and alloy industrial products, Revere had a division that made popular cookware known as Revere Ware—later breaking off as a separate manufacturing firm based in Illinois. Revere's manufacturing plant in Rome is now an employee-owned firm. During World War II, significant manufacturing capacity at Revere was turned to the making of rocket cases and bombs, and weapons manufacturing re-emerged at the plant during the Korean and Vietnam Wars.

Rome Cable Corporation, founded in 1936, was a substantial employer in the region for decades. Several other small manufacturing firms provided jobs for parents and older siblings of my friends and classmates, as did its downtown and strip mall retailers, the *Rome Daily Sentinel*, the Jervis Public Library, the schools and city and county government.

Downtown Rome was home to a movie theater, and teenagers like me could meet their friends at the Town Park and walk to the movies together. An outing with friends might also include a stop for pizza, Pepsi and ice cream at the diner on Dominick Street, followed by a couple of games at the bowling alley.

Not far from the center of town was the campus of the New York State School for the Deaf, originally established in 1875 by a deaf man named Alphonso Johnson with the support of business leaders in the city. By 1963, it had become a state-owned facility, and the infusion of millions in state funding led to the construction of a 17-acre campus on Turin Street focused on bringing innovative training to those who had difficulties with hearing and speaking. The School for the Deaf provided internships for some of my friends, and fostered an interest in careers in speech, occupational and physical therapy for many high school graduates.

On the outskirts of town, the state operated a fish hatchery and, further out, a state park that surrounded Lake Delta and provided local youngsters and their parents with a beach, hiking trails and wooded picnic areas. In nearby Westernville, a downhill ski slope provided winter recreation as did a large skating rink within the city limits.

The Rome Memorial Hospital employed many area doctors and nurses and offered a broad range of emergency and other medical care. The Rome Nursing Home on Floyd Avenue opened in 1966.

But another type of medical facility just outside the city limits hovers over Rome and other nearby communities. Institutions for those deemed to be insane were based in nearby Utica and Marcy, New York. The "Utica Lunatic Asylum," as it was originally named when opened in 1843, was one of the nation's first treatment centers for the mentally ill. On the New York Traveler website, where photos of the asylum buildings now listed on the National Register of Historic Places are showcased, a visitor in 2009 wrote:

D Riley on Wed, 15th Apr 2009 10:14 am

I was a patient there in the late 60s—before the state decided to throw all the old kept patients onto the streets. It was a very thriving and quite autonomous community—even had its own store, graphic arts studio, music program. The grounds were lovely–and all the buildings kept up—I was mostly in the new building as the old buildings housed the chronic patients who had been there forever. It was NOT a romantic place to be—and in the days of lobotomies and electro shock torture it was quite horrific. The treatment of the mentally ill has been and still in many cases is very barbaric. I knew patients who had had their brains operated on and who were never able to function again— and patients who were given shock treatments without any anesthetic and who suffered from horrific fear and nightmares the rest of their lives. Patients were also experimented on with experimental drugs and often had their nervous systems destroyed by this. It was not a fun place to be nor is its history something to be proud of. The majesty of the buildings belies the horrific events that occurred within.[24]

The environment of a region is often strongly colored by the presence of institutions such as asylums and prisons. And perspectives on mental health become warped when the names and identities of facilities allegedly intended for treating mental illness are swapped back and forth over time with those intended for incarcerating criminal perpetrators. Unfortunately, this is the story of far too many facilities in American history. The very term "Marcy" invoked fear and ridicule among the youth of Rome, New York, when I was growing up there.

HOME ALONE WITH MOM & DAD

IN JUNE 1966, MY SISTER BETTY graduated from Rome Catholic High School (RCH). That fall, I went with my mother when we drove Betty and her belongings to Buffalo State College.

By this time, Betty and I were the only children that still required financial support. Joan was now married with one child, Carol was working as a school teacher, Diane had a graduate assistantship and was living in NYC, and Dick, who had finished high school in 1962 and technical school in 1964, was married with two children and earning good money in a factory after deciding that working for my father in a grocery store was too confining.

While Mom and I took off on what was to me a grand adventure, my father as usual was working at his store, earning the money that would help to support Betty through college while meeting our living expenses.

The three of us did things I had never done before with my mother. We went to the movies and saw the James Bond film *Goldfinger*, a very risqué experience for my then 53-year-old mother, who was more innocent than most 10-year-old girls are today. We went to the artsy Allentown section of Buffalo and heard live poets at a coffeehouse. At the age of 12, I had dressed up as a beatnik for Halloween, and here, just two years later, I encountered what appeared to me as real beatniks. We went to a folk Mass with songs and prayers in English instead of Latin on Sunday, witnessing the full impact of Vatican II and the now deceased Pope John XXIII.

Soon after Mom and I left Betty in Buffalo, I began my freshman year of high school. Rome Catholic High (RCH) was just a three-block walk from our white cape cod house with shutters the color of the blue sky. It was also a short walk to St. Paul's Church, where the more affluent, less-ethnic Catholics in Rome attended church. This was also the church of the career air force officers who were stationed at Griffiss AFB during the Vietnam War, which was in full swing that fall, with Lyndon Baines Johnson as President and Robert McNamara as Secretary of Defense.

As a freshman, I saw RCH as a brand-new large building with long halls filled with strangers and occasional familiar faces. Students from all the Catholic K-8 schools in Rome mingled with the Italian Catholics, who usually came to RCH from the public middle school. Rome Catholic High seemed like a large social world to navigate, especially when I was a freshman and I had never known any of the upperclassmen, having moved to Rome just two years before.

The Sisters who taught most of the classes were from the order of St. Joseph and were known for their work in education and health care. The priests were Franciscans who opted for education instead of leading a parish.

For most of my high school years, I was a happy and outgoing—if serious—teenager. From the minute I stepped into high school, I knew I would distinguish myself as one of the "straighter" kids, but at the same time I was a wannabee wild child. It wasn't difficult for the more "advanced" girls like Julie or Chris to convince me, for example, that I should wear more makeup, and try to shed the overly sweet Catholic image of St. Mary's middle-school years.

But even though I learned how to put on mascara, skin toner and blush, I still pushed to be a model student, cheerleader, singer in the glee club, actress in school plays and member of the honor society. In short, for all outward purposes, I was a teenager who would make any parent extremely proud and give them no worries.

During those years, with his own store and home, my father gradually began to change. Dick had disappointed him when he decided that he and his wife would leave Rome and return to East Syracuse. Dad had hoped to pass on this business he had successfully built, but Dick found it impossible to work for our father, partly due to Dad's critical nature.

Each night when he came home from the store, my mother prepared dinner with the best cut of red meat my father had available that day, along with white potatoes mashed, boiled or baked, and frozen vegetables, all served with glasses of milk. Sometimes there was a salad of iceberg lettuce, celery and tomatoes, all finely chopped. I helped to make the salad, set the table and clean up.

Dad expected Mom and me to wait on him while he pulled the TV set to the edge of the dining room to watch the CBS Evening News with Walter Cronkite, or the NBC News with Huntley and Brinkley. Every night there was news of the war in Vietnam, and Mom and I were not allowed to talk during the news. If I tried to discuss what I had learned at school that day, or how I was doing with cheerleading, chorus or the latest school play, I was immediately hushed.

When dinner was done, Dad retired to his recliner chair in the living room, cigarette in hand, and usually fell asleep while watching whatever sport or variety show might be on TV. The days of me combing his hair from behind the chair were long gone. Partly as a result of my becoming an adolescent, and partly due to his new-found swagger as the boss man and king of his castle, I no longer looked forward to that moment when Dad came home from work.

I went to my room or downstairs to finish any homework I had. By the time my sophomore year arrived, my parents had given me a radio and a small black-and-white TV and stereo system for my bedroom. So I tuned into my own sources of entertainment that appealed to me but not to my parents.

The radio at night flooded my ears with Motown, rock n' roll, and folk songs. Motown beat the drums of the civil rights movement by sharing African-American cultural influences with a wide, young American audience. And music by Joni Mitchell, Bob Dylan, the Beatles, Jefferson Airplane, Joan Baez, Country Joe and the Fish may have been varied in tone, style and melody, but it delivered consistent messages—question authority, challenge the status quo, subvert the dominant paradigm. TV shows such as *Star Trek, Mission Impossible, Hogan's Heroes, Get Smart, Hawaii Five-O* and *The Smothers Brothers* also offered a gateway to worlds far beyond the small-town conservative streets of Rome or East Syracuse.

The years of gathering the family in the kitchen, singing in harmony as we prepared a meal or set the table, and laughing over dinner were over.

The Stations of the Cross are images of the suffering and crucifixion of Jesus Christ that pervaded the sensibilities of the author as a devout Catholic child.

Fred E. Wagner bought the business of this former Mohican full-service grocery store in Rome, NY, in 1964 and renamed it Mohegan Market before the incursion of large supermarket chains.

This

GODLESS COMMUNISM

COMMUNISM! WHAT IS IT? HOW DID IT GET STARTED? WHERE IS IT GO-ING? THIS SCHOOL YEAR WE ARE GOING TO SEE WHAT MAKES COMMUNISM "TICK" BY TAKING A LOOK AT THE MAIN PARTS OF ITS HISTORY---- WITH PARTICULAR EMPHASIS ON ITS HISTORY IN RUSSIA.

NOVEMBER 7, 1917---- COMMUNISTS SEIZE PETROGRAD.

MODERN COMMUNISM GOT ITS FIRST TOEHOLD IN RUSSIA THROUGH VIOLENCE AND BLOODSHED. A REVOLUTION WAS DIRECTED BY A SMALL GROUP OF MEN WHO URGED THE PEOPLE TO ATTACK THEIR REPRESENTATIVE GOVERNMENT. THE PEOPLE DID SO BECAUSE THEY THOUGHT THE COM-MUNISTS WOULD HELP THEM LEAD A MORE COMFORTABLE LIFE. THE PEOPLE DID NOT REALIZE THAT FOR THIS PROMISE OF AN EASIER LIFE THEY WERE GIVING UP THEIR FREEDOM!

1

"This Godless Communism," *Treasure Chest of Fun & Fact*, 1961. The
Treasure Chest of Fun & Fact was a Catholic comic book published by
George A. Pflaum of Dayton, Ohio, and was provided to Catholic
parochial school students between 1946 and 1972.
From the Archives of the Catholic University of America.

GOOD SPELLERS — Spelling bee winners of the Rome-Oneida area are eighth graders of St. Mary's School, Linda M. Wagner, left, daughter of Mr. and Mrs. Fred E. Wagner,   , and Mary Elizabeth

They are among 33 pupils from parochial schools in the Syracuse Diocese who will participate in the Syracuse Herald-Journal spelling bee tomorrow in Lincoln High School auditorium, Syracuse.

Linda attended St. Mary's School for 7th and 8th grade after moving to Rome, NY.

The home of Fred & Eleanor Wagner in Rome, NY, 1964–1989

IV

EVOLUTION

Society's Child

Now I could understand your tears and your shame,
She called you "boy" instead of your name.
When she wouldn't let you inside,
When she turned and said
"But honey, he's not our kind."

– "Society's Child"
Janis Ian 1965

A SPECIFIC IMAGE IS USUALLY RESURRECTED in people's minds when they hear "a buxom blonde named Marilyn." But for me, this description and name evoke not a deceased movie star named Monroe, but a very-much-alive Irish Catholic friend whom I've known since kindergarten in East Syracuse.

Marilyn is the fourth of five children, all of whom have their father's tall height and broad frame and their mother's kind face and beautiful smile. She began to develop a woman's curvy body in only fourth grade, in contrast to my much later development of tiny breasts and long legs. After we entered sixth grade, something about our early adolescence drew us together as friends, along with another classmate who lived further up from my family's home on Heman Street.

Marilyn and I had attended St. Matthew's elementary school together since kindergarten in 1957. By the time we had reached sixth grade, it was 1963 and the more liberal wing of the Catholic Church in the U.S., which included the Franciscan sisters at our school and the Jesuits who taught two of my older sisters at Lemoyne College, was actively teaching its students about modern social justice. We learned that all races—black, white, red, brown or yellow—were equal children of God, that the Jews were not responsible for the death of Jesus, and that people of different faiths could meet together in an ecumenical spirit. In combating the divisive and destructive legacy of the Nazi era, Pope John XXIII and the Vatican II epoch had a profound influence on the values that Marilyn and I shared regarding the burgeoning civil rights movement of our youth.

I often stayed overnight at Marilyn's and during one of those sleepovers, I learned her family secret. Every Tuesday, when Marilyn's father got paid at his factory job, he would come home drunk. And on those nights, she would stay up in her bedroom with the covers pulled over her head, just waiting for the yelling and crashing sounds to begin, knowing that he was likely to beat her mother. But she loved her father, who would express regret and apologies the next day. "He's a good man. I know he is," she struggled to say. "But I hate him when he's drunk. We all hate him when he's drunk."

My father was usually a jolly drunk, and I was deeply moved by the fact that Marilyn shared this tragic family stress and sorrow with me. I felt protective of her, despite her larger size and more mature physique. It helped to create a bond between us that has endured to this day.

When I learned at the end of that school year that I would be moving away during the summer to Rome, I spent as much time as I could with Marilyn, taking the bus up past her house on Park Hill to Eastwood to go to the movies or the city park and pool. My mother sometimes dropped us off at the Suburban Amusement Park where we went on rides, played games and looked for cute boys. Marilyn was the friend with whom I first explored makeup, nail polish and perfumes. I enjoyed talking with her mother who, unlike mine, was always reading a new book and was not afraid to discuss sex with her daughters.

But before the summer was done, we had moved, and I had a new universe of people to meet. Fortunately, because my brother and his young wife still lived in East Syracuse, it was easy for me to take the train and go back to visit with Marilyn every few months. And even more importantly, Marilyn became my pen-pal. We wrote long letters to each other throughout middle and high school, chronicling our adolescent lives, including favorite rock bands, books and movies, our fears and desires, and plenty of details about the boys on whom we had the latest crush.

In addition to teen talk, Marilyn and I also shared discussion about the issues that were turning the world upside down in those years. In Rome, I was being taught the doctrine of just war in religion class, while the U.S. was increasing its troop levels in Vietnam. Marilyn and I talked about morality and politics in addition to chatting about which Beatle was our favorite or which TV shows we couldn't bear to miss.

By the time Janis Ian's "Society's Child" hit the charts on Top Ten radio, Marilyn's mother had moved to an apartment to get away from her abusive husband. The next year, after Marilyn had left St. Matthew's and entered the regional public high school, she fell head over heels for a handsome black basketball player named Ed.

Ed had a cousin named Jerry, and when I visited Marilyn that fall, we "double-dated" at her mother's apartment while her mom was at work and her younger brother was out visiting friends. In the room where Marilyn slept, there were two twin beds; she climbed into one with Ed and I went into the other with Jerry. Ed and Jerry were gentle and kind, and while Ed may have gone to second or third base with Marilyn, Jerry did no more than kiss me sweetly and shyly during our encounter.

Marilyn and I hid our relationships with Ed and Jerry from our parents, but the experience led me to bring up a key question to my father one evening at the dinner table.

"What would you do if I had a boyfriend who was black?" I prodded.

He answered, "I'd ground you." His eyes gave me a glare I had never seen before.

"But what if we were all grown up, and he had a good job, and we were in love and wanted to get married?"

"I wouldn't be at that wedding. End of discussion," he said and abruptly got up and walked away to sit in front of the TV in the living room.

Although I suspected that Dad might feel this way, I was stunned and ashamed to hear the words come out of his mouth. I sat there with my jaw dropped open while my mother hummed a tune as she cleaned up the kitchen. Two of my older sisters, who believed in racial equality as I did, had dated African foreign students during their college years and had confronted this racism in our home several years earlier.

But this was the first time I came to see my father as a bigot. I knew that Jerry was a bright, gentle and intelligent boy who had big plans for his future. Without consideration of the color of his skin—which was light compared to Ed's—he was just the type of young man a father should hope would be interested in his daughter.

The charm that my father had held for me when I was a child began to erode on that night. Every time that I saw a news clip of Martin Luther King Junior leading a civil rights march, or watched Nat King Cole on a variety show, or heard The Supremes on the radio, it reminded me of my affection for Jerry and the bitter wall of hatred I had faced in my father. When the streets were burning with riots in Buffalo the following year, I understood the reasons and empathized with the young black rioters instead of the small business owners, similar to my father, whose livelihoods had gone up in flames.

FATHER STEPHAN

Entering Rome Catholic High School in September 1966, all sections of the freshmen in my class had Father Bernard Stephan as their English teacher. During our sophomore year, we had a nun as our English teacher, but by our junior and senior years, Father Stephan was reassigned to us. As a result, he became the teacher we knew and loved best, and who loved us in return.

Father Stephan noticed the female gender, but in a respectful, if surprising, way for a teacher and a priest. One of the first days of our freshman year, he entered the classroom after all of us were seated and noticeably sniffed the air.

"I detect a nice cologne." He walked around, sniffing the air. "Generoso," (he always called us by our last names), is that you?"

As freshman girls in that place and time, many of us were wearing some type of scent. But Chris Generoso had one of the more mature female bodies in our class, and her flirtatious style was apparent to anyone who walked around our school halls. She also wore plenty of perfume.

"Excuse me?" Chris asked, in her deep, gravelly voice.

"Is that your perfume I smell?"

"I don't know. It's Windsong." She lifted her wrist up and he sniffed.

"Yes, that's it. You must think it odd that I would notice, but I've come here from an all-boys school, where the classes often smelled like locker rooms."

The entire class giggled and made faces, and Father Stephan quickly moved on to a discussion of *The Red Badge of Courage*. Steph, as we called him, was a demanding teacher but he knew how to kid around and engage with us while pushing us to do our best work.

I think it was during our sophomore year that one of us asked Father Stephan after class one day why he had entered the priesthood. Just a few of us had remained behind to ask a few questions and by then, Chris had admitted to me and some of the other girls that she had a crush on him. When she talked about him, she often began singing "To Sir, with Love" from the 1967 movie with that name starring Sidney Poitier.

I recall a significant shift in Father Stephan's body language and an uncharacteristic expression that I had never seen in him before. He always presented a crusty and tough exterior to us in class—making it clear that he was in control—but this expression seemed an odd cross between anger, pain and sorrow. He pursed his lips as if eating a lemon, breathed in deeply and then let out a long sigh.

"This is not a story I like to share. But since you've asked, and you're old enough to understand, I'll tell you about it. When I first got out of high school, I went into the seminary. But somewhere along my way, I met a lovely young woman and fell in love. I left the seminary and eventually, I asked her to marry me and amazingly, she said yes. But about a month before our wedding, she was killed in a car crash."

Other than the audible gasps when these words first came out of his mouth, our small group grew as still and quiet as a winter landscape in northern Canada.

"I took this as a sign from God that he wanted me to become a priest. I went back into the seminary and here I am."

Lucky for us, the bell rang as he finished the story. While we were old enough to understand, we were not mature enough to know how to respond to this heartbreaking story, the likes of which we had never heard from any teacher before in our lives. Most of the time, we did not see teachers—especially not priests and nuns—as regular human beings.

I stayed in the room for just a few moments more and said, "I'm so sorry." And then we moved on quickly to our next class.

CHRIS, ANNE AND VODKA

CHRIS AND I BOTH MADE THE cheerleading squad in our freshman year and we became friends that year. She was much more outgoing and outspoken than me, and we shared a deep and abiding love of family. Like me and another classmate, Patricia, Chris liked to sing. The three of us would sing in harmony in the hallways between classes at Rome Catholic High. At home, Chris' favorite singers included Barbara Streisand and Frank Sinatra—I was more a fan of the current Top 40, but I also liked other tunes from the American Songbook of the 1940s and early 1950s that my sisters had sung when I was younger.

In addition to Chris, I became good friends with some of the more intellectual and creative girls—Bonne, Joan, Barb—we shared a love of Simon and Garfunkel tunes and a belief in the Catholic faith. Bonne was in all of my classes and Joan and Barb were cheerleading buddies, along with Kathy, Bernadette and the Christopher twins. This was my circle of good Catholic girlfriends; we acted silly together, sang songs in French and shared who was our favorite Beatle. With all of these girls, I engaged in healthy activities, such as skating, bowling, skiing, and Catholic Youth Organization (CYO) trips, including to the Expo '67 World's Fair in Montreal. When we got together, the only thing we drank was soda pop, and our riskiest activity was the use of a Ouija Board to predict the future.

But in addition to wholesome, innocent, fun-packed activities with my plentiful crowd of good girls, I began to embrace a riskier and more socially critical side of life with a different circle of friends and acquaintances. At some time during that year, Chris introduced me to her neighborhood friend Anne, who lived just down the block from her on Healy Ave. Anne was also Catholic, but she went to Rome Free Academy, the public high school, and she was a year ahead of us.

Anne and I shared a growing political skepticism about the Vietnam War, the role of the Catholic Church, and the narrow-mindedness and colorless nature of the dominant American culture. We were intrigued by protest and countercultural music that flooded the radio waves and the newly prevailing fashion of army/navy greens and blues that implied a love/hate relationship with country and military. When I stayed overnight at her house, we talked endlessly about books, history and politics as well as boys.

The first time I ever drank alcohol, I was at Anne's house for a sleepover with Chris during the summer between our freshman and sophomore years. Anne had done the timeworn trick of teen boozers—she had taken vodka from her parents' cabinet while they were out. After pouring some of the vodka into another container to mix with orange juice, she took the bottle to the sink and filled it with water back up to the line where the vodka had been. She shook it up and put it back in the cabinet.

I was afraid to drink the liquor and I said so. But Anne and Chris had done it before, and they assured me it would be a lot of fun and that no one else would ever find out. The latter part was true—no one else ever learned about that night. But after drinking several tumbler glasses of Screwdrivers with a heavy concentration of vodka, which did not taste as bad as I had expected, my head started to spin. I began to cry in near hysteria, sobbing, "God is going to hate me for doing this. I'm so terrible. My parents are going to find out and they'll be so disappointed. I was so stupid to do this. I'm a sinner."

Chris and Anne took turns trying to comfort me, but Chris was too drunk to be of much help. Soon she ran into the bathroom and vomited. After helping Chris to clean herself up, Anne tucked her into bed. Then she came back into the kitchen where I had laid my head down on the table, worn out from crying.

"Linda, you're not a bad person," Anne said to me as she put her arm around my shoulder and stroked my hair like my sisters did when I was little. "A lot of people get drunk. You're just not used to it. You have to build up a tolerance for it."

We went into the living room and listened to music by The Doors.

> You know the day destroys the night
> Night divides the day
> Tried to run
> Tried to hide
> Break on through to the other side…[25]

As the songs played on, Anne kept talking about her feelings for Jimmy—the guitarist in a rock band in her neighborhood. After I fell asleep on the living room floor, she woke me up and helped me get into the sleeping bag on the floor in her room. The next morning I woke up late with a headache, but I could see that the wrath of God had not descended upon me. After some breakfast and coffee, the three of us laughed and laughed about the night before, describing to each other the crazy things we had done and said.

After that episode, I drank alcohol a little more slowly. When cheerleading at high school football or basketball games was done for the evening, I'd go out on the streets with some of the cheerleaders and drink a couple of beers. I rarely got as drunk again as I had that first night at Anne's house but I did sneak liquor from my father's bar in the basement den once in a while when I had some of my more risk-enjoying friends at the house for sleepovers.

Not once did my parents ever suspect that I was drinking. At least, they never said anything to me if they did. Little did they know, I had been drinking for more than two years by the time I began to engage in what they eventually saw as riskier behaviors.

THE ACCEPTABLE BOYFRIEND

Tom C. Ryan was a blond, year-round athlete, one of the best in our school, with above-average but not egghead grades, a winning smile, a fun attitude and what girls our age considered a great "bod." Not surprisingly, he was in demand and just as I developed a crush on him, Chris wooed and won him. They dated for a while, but as was Chris' trademark in those years, she flirted with the other guys and soon found an upperclassman to take her out. Tom considered the popular song "Spooky" to be hers, especially the lyrics, "You always keep me guessing, I just never seem to know what you are thinking. And if a fella looks at you, it's for sure your little eye'll be a winking."

It was some time after Chris and Tom broke up, late in our freshman year in high school, that a classmate held a party across from the city's main park. The parents weren't home, the lights were low, and there were a lot of kissing games going on. I'm not sure how it started, but before long, I found myself on the floor with Tom, making out and feeling desires I had never before known. After that night, Tom and I were an off-and-on item, going to the movies together, and meeting at his house when nobody was home. We would spend an hour or more on the phone in the evening, with Tom doing most of the talking. I was completely smitten and filled with longing to be with him all the time.

In an era that has gone well beyond the sexual revolution of the 1960s to the likes of Miley Cyrus, it's hard to fathom today what the pressures were on a 15-year-old Catholic girl in 1967. Having attended Catholic school since kindergarten, taught by nuns from the age of four-and-a-half, I had heard the stories of the female saints over and over by that time. Except for Joan of Arc, it was always the same story—whether it was Maria Goretti or Agatha, the saint was a young woman who was pushed by some man to "give in" to his carnal desires and lose her virginity, which was idolized in the form of the Virgin Mary, mother of Jesus. The saint always held out, either insisting that sex was only permissible for procreation within the sacrament of marriage, or vowing that she intended to join a convent and dedicate her life to the Lord, becoming forever a virgin bride to Jesus. Inevitably, the evil man would steal her virginity and then kill her, leading to her canonization and to the underlying message that sex outside of marriage is an evil that leads to death.

This was powerful imagery for an impressionable child. In me and countless other young Catholic girls, it merged with the ingrained belief that it was a mortal sin for females to give in to sexual desire and with fears of pregnancy, shame and irreversible harm to your reputation. By giving in, you risked the label of "slut," "whore," or in Rome, New York, the Italian-American vernacular "puttana."

And so, despite a desperate longing to tear off my clothes and consummate the lust I felt, I maintained what I thought was a purer form of love for Tom, telling him he would lose respect for me forever if I gave in and went all the way with him. Before long, on a weekend night when Tom said he was going out with the boys, he ended up at Chris' house, drunk and horny. To her credit, Chris called me the next day, told me he had come over, and she confessed that she had let him make out with her.

It was the first time I fully recognized the emotional impact of betrayal, tinged with anger, sorrow and feelings of abandonment and humiliation; my heart had been broken by my boyfriend and one of my best friends. The warpath percussive rhythm of "I Heard It Through the Grapevine," followed by the sorrowful melody of "The Tennessee Waltz," droned on over and over in my mind. I stopped talking to Tom and began avoiding Chris.

At the end of the school year, when our yearbooks came out, I asked Tom to sign mine. He wrote, "You were the best I had and I blew it." I thought there might be a chance to revive our relationship until I learned later that week that Tom's family was moving far away. The Rome Cable Company was shutting down operations in New York State and moving them to a small town in Illinois where his father was being transferred, since the costs of business were cheaper there. Tom decided that he should spend his remaining time in Rome with a broad range of his friends and that reigniting our relationship was futile, given the distance. Once again, my heart was torn apart and for weeks, I sobbed into my pillow every night until I fell asleep.

JUST WAR

Tell her to reap it in a sickle of leather
War bellows, blazing in scarlet battalions
Parsley, sage, rosemary, and thyme
Generals order their soldiers to kill
And to gather it all in a bunch of heather
And to fight for a cause they've long ago forgotten
Then she'll be a true love of mine.

– "Scarborough Fair/Canticle" Traditional
& Paul Simon/Art Garfunkel 1966

AT SOME POINT DURING MY FRESHMAN year in high school in 1966–'67, the national tensions about the Vietnam War became evident to me and to most of the rest of the country. There are few places in the U.S. where internal debate over American military involvement becomes more hostile than in a community with a military installation, such as Griffiss Air Force Base. And since the Catholic career officers at Griffiss sent their children to Rome Catholic High, the moral debate at my school was keen.

Father Timothy Boyle was a young, kind and gentle priest with a winning smile and brilliant blue eyes. He was a good choice as a religion teacher of high school freshmen, since his youthful demeanor and spirit were inviting rather than alienating. Unlike some of the more militaristic priests at RCH, he leaned toward pacifism, sharing with his students a love for Simon and Garfunkel's album, *The Sounds of Silence*. It was left to Father Boyle to teach the Catholic doctrine of just war, which originated with St. Augustine and was refined by St. Thomas Aquinas during the 13th century.

According to Catholic Answers, the foremost website for all Catholic answers and topics, "The most authoritative and up-to-date expression of just war doctrine is found in paragraph 2309 of the Catechism of the Catholic Church." It goes on to further define just what conditions are necessary for military force.

> The strict conditions for legitimate defense by military force require rigorous consideration. The gravity of such a decision makes it subject to rigorous conditions of moral legitimacy. At one and the same time:
> - the damage inflicted by the aggressor on the nation or community of nations must be lasting, grave, and certain;
> - all other means of putting an end to it must have been shown to be impractical or ineffective;
> - there must be serious prospects of success;
> - the use of arms must not produce evils and disorders graver than the evil to be eliminated. The power of modern means of destruction weighs very heavily in evaluating this condition.
>
> These are the traditional elements enumerated in what is called the "just war" doctrine. The evaluation of these conditions for moral legitimacy belongs to the prudential judgment of those who have responsibility for the common good.[26]

In our Catholic doctrine classes, Father Boyle presented the Church teaching and then asked, "So what do you think about this teaching? Do you think it was a good description for why the U.S. fought against the Nazis in World War II? Patricia, you haven't said a word yet. What do you think about that?"

Pat, who was in my homeroom class, was generally quiet but she responded quickly to this question. "My father and my uncle fought in World War II, and I think it was the most just war in history. The Nazis were evil and we had to fight them to save Europe."

"OK, that's a good answer Patricia. So what about the Korean War? Did anyone have relatives who fought in that war?

A few people raised their hand, but the class was quiet when Father Boyle asked the natural follow-up, "Four people had relatives who fought in the Korean War. Do you think that war met the definition that we have of a just war? Come on now, speak up. Mark, what about you? Do you think that was a just war?"

"I'm sure my cousin wouldn't have gone over there to fight it if it wasn't fair and square," Mark replied.

"What about the German soldiers who fought for Hitler in World War II? Do you think that if someone answers the call of their country to go to war, that makes it a just war?" Father Boyle prodded.

I raised my hand. "Linda, go ahead."

"A lot of Americans are going to fight in Vietnam, but that doesn't seem to be a just war, the way you explained it."

"What makes you say that?"

"What did they do to us? They didn't attack us or anything. Couldn't we find a more peaceful way to approach them? After all, we have the United Nations now."

A couple of other people piped in, "Yeah. That's right."

The son of an Air Force captain raised his hand, and Father Boyle called on him.

"Just because a war isn't popular, that doesn't mean it's not just. If we don't stop the Communists in Vietnam, they'll be knocking on our doors in a few years and you won't be able to have religion classes like this at all anymore."

Father Boyle raised his eyebrows as the class broke into a noisy internal debate. "OK, OK, that's enough. Richard makes a valid point. But it's good to have a healthy debate before we send our young people off to fight any war. Sometimes it's not right to follow orders, as we saw with the Nazi soldiers during World War II. We'll continue the discussion in the next class."

Many of us, as with peace activists such as Father Daniel Berrigan and his brother Philip, did not see the U.S. involvement as morally legitimate. Vietnam had not attacked the U.S., and we believed there were other ways to address our differences with the Vietnamese. We saw no chance of success in the conflict, and we saw U.S. forces commit atrocities right from our TV sets. On all four counts of the "just war" doctrine, the American war in Vietnam seemed clearly unjustified. What's more, we had friends who were subject to a draft, and we did not want their lives turned into cannon fodder, only adding to the piles of young American and Vietnamese lives that had already been lost.

The Roman Catholic Church did not interpret the war in the same light, and my fellow students who were the sons of Air Force officers argued with Father Boyle, me and anyone else throughout our high school years that the Church's view was the correct view: the Church and the U.S. government and military were locked together in a righteous battle against godless Communism that threatened to overtake the world if we allowed the domino of Vietnam to fall.

Missing from both sides of these arguments were facts about the history of the Catholic Church itself within Vietnam. This history is controversial but long; some claim that the Roman Catholic Church manipulated the U.S. into the war and that Catholic officials in South Vietnam viciously discriminated against Buddhists. There is evidence that some 16th and 17th century missionary priests became military strategists in Vietnam.

The Catholic Reporter, in an April 24, 2003 article titled "Vietnam's 400-year Catholic History," acknowledged that the history of the Church's involvement in Vietnam was far longer than that of the U.S. or France.

> Coming to Vietnam after Buddhism, Catholicism has developed for 400 years or so. Right from its first days on this land, this religion was exploited by the French colonialists in their scheme to occupy Vietnam and many missionaries played an important role in its implementation. At various stages Catholic armed units assisted French colonial forces to oppose national liberation movements. However, many Catholics also joined resistance forces against French colonialism.
>
> In 1954 when Vietnam was divided, many anti-communist Catholics came south and became the mainstay behind Ngo Dinh Diem and the South Vietnamese government. When the country was united in 1975 many Catholics were treated with suspicion by the new government. Slowly since then Catholics and the Communist-led government have been working out a rapprochement.[27]

With a 400-year history in Vietnam, it would not be surprising that the Catholic Church had its own interests to protect there, long before the U.S. military arrived. What this had to do with American involvement in the Vietnam War is difficult to untangle.

But if I and other Catholic high school students had been taught the somewhat sordid history of Catholic priests and Vietnamese military history, we may not have been so puzzled about why the Church did not condemn the American war there as unjust. Of course, if we had learned about the Church's own failures to meet the "just war" test throughout history, some of us might have questioned Catholic teachings sooner and more deeply.

But even without knowing that history, I became more and more troubled and disillusioned about the discrepancy between what I had learned about the "just war" doctrine and the way that my country had grown entangled in a southeast Asian civil war. And since I was the daughter of a grocer and not an Air Force man, I had not been indoctrinated by the same ideological military rationale that many of my classmates and some teachers with military experience had.

I was growing out of step with the dominant paradigm, at home and at school. At the same time, I was more and more susceptible to the influences of a rising counterculture.

DOUBT

My own deep doubts about Catholicism had begun during my sophomore year of high school when I had an encounter in my daily religious doctrine class with Father Fallon, a red-headed Irish priest with a strong passion for papal infallibility. After his class lecture, Father Fallon would do his best—as did Father Boyle the previous year—to engage us in discussion and I was usually a ready participant. One day, during a class about the behaviors that would most certainly land a soul in heaven or hell, I earnestly said, "Guardian angels were a great invention for children to help them feel that they'll be protected when their parents aren't around. But as we get older, we grow beyond them, like we outgrow Santa Claus."

Father Fallon's face turned a deep crimson red that clashed with his orange-red hair, and the veins on his neck stood out as he screamed at me, "Ms. Wagner, that is heresy! Guardian angels are not something we 'grow out of.' They are a fact of Catholic life and you'd better believe in them."

Once again, I was saved by the bell, but shaken to hear that this priest actually thought I would suffer eternal damnation because I had trouble believing in the reality of heavenly creatures with wings sitting on my shoulder. By the age of 13 or 14, what seemed to me a comforting bedtime tale for children, who had not yet reached the age of reason, had become only a myth that ran counter to what I felt was a deeper sense of spirituality.

On the home front, the reality that came into our living room every night on the TV news only eroded my faith more and more as my teen years went by. I watched the coverage in October 1967 when my favorite folk singer, Joan Baez, was arrested for a peaceful protest against the military draft. That November, I saw President Lyndon Johnson lash out at pro-testers during an address to the nation. I saw irony when the news covered space-crafts heading for the moon right after stories about American cities being torched by impoverished, disaffected minorities.

In addition, neither of my parents seemed to have any idea that I was gradually developing a bitter anger at my father. Un-like the years when I was an innocent child in East Syracuse and would run to greet Dad every night when he came home from work, I was now the only child at home and things had changed. In the morning at the breakfast table, my father would plant sloppy kisses on my neck and make nasty old man snort-ing noises, implying that I was sexually desirable. But I did not take this as a compliment and instead, it made me both con-fused and furious. I was humiliated and frightened when he was drunk one night and made me sit on his lap in the living room, until my mother reminded him, "Fred, she's your daughter."

My mother worked at the store with my father during the day, handling the bookkeeping, and came home earlier than him and started dinner every night. If she had made a mistake in her bookkeeping, he would relentlessly ask, "How could you be so stupid?" If she did not broil a steak to perfection, he would taunt her inept cooking and complain, "Once again El, you've ru-ined an excellent cut of meat." It was obvious to everyone at the store, including me who sometimes worked in the bakery, that he found one of his employees, a younger divorcee named Jenny, very fetching. At home, he would frequently tell my mother, his wife of 30 years, "You're ugly."

I've worked hard to forgive my father for this verbal abuse of my mother, knowing now that he was an undiagnosed diabetic in those years, a condition that can lead to mood swings. But at the age of 16, I felt that Dad's conduct had become just one more reason to rebel against the prevailing order.

YOUTH LEADERSHIP AND THE ODD SPEAKER

IN MY JUNIOR YEAR OF HIGH school, I traveled to Syracuse to participate in a young leaders conference. The invitation to this event was an honor in New York State awarded to students who had excelled in the study of American history.

One of the speakers at the day-long event was a psychiatrist scheduled to speak to this large gathering of teenagers about the dangers of alcohol and substance abuse.

It was the spring of 1969, and the doctor's audience was filled with young people of promise—bright, well-educated and generally, quite serious. But given the times, surrounded by political and cultural upheaval, many intelligent teens were very skeptical of authority.

I remember chatting with other students I had just met that day, all of us wondering what scare tactics would be used to warn us of the dangers of the drug culture. I had done my share of drinking booze by that time, but I had never smoked pot or taken any other types of drugs. The films we saw in health education and science classes were like bad Grade B horror films, and we chuckled together while recalling scenes of crazed teenagers and maudlin music.

But no joking around could have prepared us for the bizarre man who spoke in a thick Cuban accent about wild animals drinking fermented juices off the jungle floor and acting strangely. The entire room full of students found this speaker to be a ridiculous curiosity whose talk ambled and wandered, as did our attention. Even stranger, he periodically took a small bottle out of his inside jacket pocket and snorted whatever spray it contained.

We looked at each other in puzzled disbelief at this alleged expert who seemed like a buffoon with no clue how to communicate with an audience of young American high-school student leaders. Some of the kids whispered that he must be a junkie himself since he couldn't stop snorting from that bottle he kept pulling out of his jacket pocket.

We managed to contain ourselves to quiet snickers while he spoke, but when he finished, we burst into laughter and tried to cover it with applause.

Little did I know at the time that, before I finished high school, I would come under the control of this seemingly eccentric doctor.

* * *

The odd doctor who spoke to me and other high school students at the Young Leaders conference in 1969 had been working as a psychopharmacological researcher in central New York State for more than 10 years. Anthony Sainz began his work at Marcy State Hospital near Utica in September 1955, while I was about to turn three years old just 50 miles away in East Syracuse. By that time my Aunt Leona, who, according to my siblings, was initially hospitalized at Marcy in the 1920s, had been living at Willard State Hospital in the Finger Lakes region for more than two decades.

If she had lived in a state mental hospital in several other states, and her behavior was viewed as so unruly that it warranted further control, Aunt Leona might have been given a frontal lobe lobotomy or sterilization surgery. Fortunately for Leona, such surgical interventions were not the norm in New York's hospitals.

But they were not uncommon in Iowa, where Dr. Anthony Sainz had practiced psychiatry. By September 1950, according to the April 22, 1954 edition of *The Laurens Sun* newspaper in Laurens, Iowa, Dr. Anthony Sainz was a resident psychiatrist at the Cherokee Iowa Mental Health Institute, otherwise known as the Cherokee State Hospital. He worked there with Dr. D. E. Wynegar until Wynegar accepted a post with the VA Hospital in Omaha, at which time Sainz was appointed to head the Outpatient Clinic.[28]

In the late spring of 1951, the public was invited to tour Cherokee State Hospital, in an apparent effort to alleviate the concerns about state mental facilities that Albert Deutsch had raised in the late 1940s with his book *The Shame of the States*. An article about the tour of this "City of the Sick" published in an Iowa newspaper in late May 1951 reported, "Over half the hospital beds in the U.S. are occupied by mental patients, about 600,000. From 30 to 60% of all the patients consulting doctors do so primarily for complaints due to emotional disorders."[29]

With credibility endowed by his newly reported titles of Acting Assistant Superintendent and Clinical Director at Cherokee, Dr. Sainz embarked on a two-decade-long path of public speaking on mental health topics to women's clubs and other civic groups. Many of his engagements were reported in local newspapers of the 1950s and 1960s, first in Iowa and later in New York. Some talks were titled, "Your Vital Child," "Drugs and Therapy in Treatment of Mental Illness," and "Emotional Health and Adjustment." In November 1954, a film he made entitled, *The Angry Boy*, accompanied his talk.[30]

In a March 13, 1953 article in the *Cedar Rapids Gazette*, Sainz extols the value of transorbital and prefrontal lobotomies that had been performed at the Cherokee Institute. In one paragraph he is quoted as claiming that the procedures "have resulted in social recovery of 35 percent of the operated patients." Later, that same article says, "Sainz said the prefrontal and transorbital lobotomies have resulted in improvement in about 60 percent of patients here." It goes on to announce that an "amygdaloidectomy" had been performed there the previous Wednesday, the sixth of its kind "since its inception by Walter Freeman, outstanding neuropathologist who also perfected techniques of prefrontal and transorbital lobotomies." Freeman was the co-author of a journal article, "Amygdaloidectomy for the suppression of auditory hallucinations; a preliminary report of a theory and its application in one case."[31]

A 2008 documentary titled *The Lobotomist* produced by the U.S. Public Broadcasting Series "The American Experience," chronicled Freeman's lobotomies in shocking detail, with historic video footage of the procedure. Patients were strapped down and given electroshock until they were rendered unconscious. Then an ice pick—or a surgical tool modeled after an ice pick—was inserted into the eye socket above the eyeball to sever a part of the brain. After the procedure, patients were given dark glasses to cover the black eyes received during the course of the surgery.[32] Many of the procedures were done outside of a typical surgical setting, and patients were often sent on their way home or back to a state mental facility immediately after the brain surgery. The most famous patient was a sister of President John F. Kennedy.

Freeman's history of lobotomy "road trips" to state hospitals around the U.S. was also chronicled in a *Washington Post* article by journalist Jack El-Hai, on February 4, 2001.[33] A number of

Freeman's patients died or were rendered permanently disabled between the 1930s and 1960s. One death in 1967 resulted in a loss of Freeman's hospital privileges and the end to his lobotomy practice. The *Post* article also notes how Freeman bragged that he had figured out how to gain press accolades, despite his questionable results. A 1952 Associated Press news article reporting on a plan for mass lobotomies on West Virginia state mental patients renders both praise and doubt, noting that even at that time, "Not all mental specialists agree it is a good idea. Some of them say it does more harm than good. A section of the brain is damaged beyond repair."[34]

Despite the doubts of others in the profession, the association between Sainz and Freeman in the early 1950s seemed to benefit Sainz. The headline of an article in *The Democrat* newspaper in March 19, 1953, refers to Sainz as the "Famed Medic of Cherokee." Several other articles refer to him as "a leading psychiatrist in the country."[35]

But by the end of 1953, Sainz had stopped singing the praises of surgical lobotomies and began promoting his own research on psychotropic drugs. He played a notable role in what passed, from the mid-1950s until the early 1970s, as credible research on such pharmaceuticals as Chlorpromazine, Reserpine, Phenothiazine, "diphenyl" derivatives, "phrenopraxic" drugs, diethazine, ethopropazine, ahlorpromazine, mepazine, Phenelzine, and Methonalide, according to professional psychiatric journals of the 1950s and 1960s. Newspaper articles also cite research conducted at Marcy State Hospital while Sainz headed the Research Division there on drugs such as "Thorazine and Librium, both tranquilizers, Nardil, an anti-depressant, and Proketazine, an anti-depressant for schizophrenics," and the psychiatric action of antihistamines.[36]

Later in the 1950s, it is more than likely that my Aunt Leona and her fellow patients at Willard and other state hospitals around the U.S. were being given new pharmaceutical products that were viewed by doctors such as Anthony Sainz as more humane than previous treatments. Clearly, the new drugs that were considered to be a type of *chemical* or "medicinal" lobotomy were far less messy than the surgical lobotomies performed by Freeman with an ice pick tool, such as those given to more than 40,000 residents of American state mental hospitals in the decades just prior to the mid-1950s.[37]

But as any high jumper can tell you, it is relatively easy to surpass a bar that is set so low.

The civil rights movement was a central political and cultural backdrop
for those growing up in the 1960s.

Simon & Garfunkel were part of the 1960s folk music revival that often
carried gently sun anti-war sentiments to young listeners.

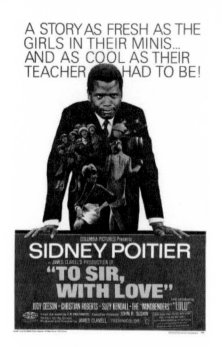

To Sir With Love was both a popular film and a number-one hit single by singer Lulu in 1967.

Linda with other Rome Catholic High cheerleaders on the bus to a basketball game in 1967.

V

REVOLUTION

HELL'S THE HIPPEST WAY TO GO

Everybody's saying that hell's the hippest way to go.
Well I don't think so,
I'm gonna take a look around it though.

– "Blue"
Joni Mitchell

FOR NEARLY EVERY TEENAGE GIRL, THE summer of your 16th year is a confusing, exciting time filled with hormonal surges and drops, intellectual leaps and climbs, and emotional sways and swings. There are few years in history when this sweet-16 chaos was amplified more than in 1969. It was the summer that the Woodstock rock festival brought a half-million young people together in a peaceful but revolutionary mood.

There were many other major happenings that impacted the U.S. that year: among them, Sirhan Sirhan admitted he killed Robert Kennedy, the Smothers Brothers Comedy Hour was cancelled when the popular satirists refused to submit to censorship, the Stonewall riots in NYC launched the gay rights movement, Charles Manson and his cult followers killed Sharon Tate and her guests, and the Chicago 8 trial opened in Chicago with defendants bound and gagged in the courtroom. Hundreds of thousands of people participated in antiwar demonstrations across the United States, while the first military-draft lottery since WWII was held in the United States. With Woodstock over, a *Rolling Stones* concert in California ended with a concert-goer stabbed to death by members of Hell's Angels, who were supposed to provide security.

On the global stage in 1969, the Beatles released their last album, Yassar Arafat took over the PLO, Golda Meir became Prime Minister of Israel, the British sent troops into Northern Ireland to quash violence there, and a coup in Libya brought Col. Moammar Qaddafi to power. A soccer match led to war between Honduras and El Salvador, and when Apollo 11 landed on the moon, Neil Armstrong took "one small step for man."[38]

Just two years earlier, in July of 1967, a *Time Magazine* cover story had announced the arrival of "The Hippies," summarizing the phenomenon with: "If there were a hippie code, it would include these flexible guidelines: Do your own thing, wherever you have to do it and whenever you want. Drop out. Leave society as you have known it. Leave it utterly. Blow the mind of every straight person you can reach. Turn them on, if not to drugs, then to beauty, love, honesty, fun."[39]

By 1969, a counterculture of folk and rock music, free love and flowers was hard to distinguish from political activism. This activism was expressed within movements for peace in Vietnam, African-American civil rights, reparations for Native Americans, women's liberation, environmental awareness and sexual freedom. Young adults—even those who had finished college at Ivy League schools—were dropping out and joining communes or other non-conformist lifestyles, wearing blue jeans and sandals rather than pursuing traditional careers with suits, ties, dresses and leather shoes.

The countercultural and anti-political tsunami that was crashing across the nation and world was visibly reaching the small city of Rome, New York. Summer nights and weekends were suffused with change that inquisitive young minds could hear, see, taste, and even smell in the sweet scent of marijuana wafting through gathered crowds.

While many of the sensations of that era were pleasurable, at the same time, many were traumatically painful. Deep fissures had emerged within American families of all races and economic groups, evidenced in such songs as "The Great Mandela" by Peter, Paul, & Mary (*What the hell does he think he's doing to his father who brought him up right?*) and "What's Going On?" by Marvin Gaye (*"Father, father, everybody thinks we're wrong, Oh, but who are they to judge us, Simply 'cause our hair is long?"*). As with youth gangs, children who were—in essence—being cast out of their homes and families sought solace, comfort and support only from their contemporaries.

For me, August 1969 was the month when I shed the insulated cocoon of American post-WWII innocence. Rather than emerge with butterfly wings to fly away, I fell into a cauldron of stewing forces I could barely comprehend. The catalyst for this fall from grace was a summer afternoon encounter with my former boyfriend, Tom, who was visiting his old hometown after moving to southern Illinois.

While I spent many weekdays that summer working in the bakery at my father's store, I spent time with friends at the local lake or out in the countryside on my days off. I was thrilled to learn that Tom would be in town and was hardly able to contain my desire. When we finally met alone, the lusty excitement that had drawn us together before had matured even further. He came to my house while my parents were at work, and after a half hour of chatting and laughing, we began to kiss, finally ending up on the couch in an embrace that quickly reached the boiling point.

Tom pushed, "Don't you want the real thing?"

The specter of Catholic girl saints merged with the fear of pregnancy and I said, "No, Tom, I can't."

"C'mon Linda, I know you want it and so do I."

"Tom, I can't, no."

I sat up on the couch as Tom got up and sat in the chair across the room, fuming silently.

"Don't you have anything to say?" I said, naively imagining that he would apologize.

"No," he said curtly and got up and walked out the door without looking back.

I was left in shock, feeling my own physical frustration combined with emotional abandonment. I sobbed and sobbed for at least an hour. But eventually, I stood up and went to my dresser drawer where I kept all the wonderful long letters he had sent me from Illinois. I gathered them together and took them outside the door of our garage with a box of kitchen matches. I piled them on the sidewalk, struck a match, and lit them on fire, ensuring that every last page and every envelope was ablaze in a flame so hot it could not be doused by the tears falling from my face.

Tom's letters were not the only things that went up in flames with my impromptu bonfire. And to be fair to Tom, his rejection of my unwillingness to give in to his sexual demand was only the final straw in a long-simmering erosion of my faith. I had lost my belief in my Church, my country, my family, even in my friends—in an entire way of life and values in American society. The next time I saw Tom a few nights later, we were out on the streets on a warm, breezy August night with dozens of other restless young people.

We both expressed our regrets that things had to end the way they did. But at the same time, we had the sense that we would move along in our separate lives while being part of the same larger currents that we couldn't name at the time. Something deep inside, some spell cast by centuries of Catholic doctrine and decades of American history, had been broken. I was 16 going on 17, no longer feeling innocent nor naïve, and I knew that our world could never be the same.

One of the first things I did to signal this shift was to smoke pot and feel for myself what Tom, Anne, Paul and many other friends were raving and giggling about. Just like my first drunken binge, I was at Anne's house the first time I "toked up" with Paul, Chris, and Chris' boyfriend Fred. It didn't take more than three turns at a joint before I said quietly, "I'm stoned."

Paul said, "How do you know?"

"I just know," I said with a wide grin. And Paul belted out his characteristic laugh that combined the joy of a child with the cunning of a fisherman who had just snared a big catch. It was a laugh both infectious and endearing, and with his mop of golden-brown hair and small, packed physique, I suddenly saw, heard and felt why he had such appeal. He had not only won me as a convert of getting high, he had played the pipes I wanted to follow. And follow I did.

THE PIED PIPER

PAUL WAS NOT SIMPLY A YOUNG man to me when I fell in love with him. He was a symbol of artistic freedom with an intriguing voice, an impish actor with a winning smile. My father distrusted him from the moment he saw him. But, trusting and gullible, I heard music and poetry when I was around Paul.

At age 19, he had dropped out of his second year at college, for reasons I never learned. And because he was at home in the boring town of Rome, New York, and not at school, he was seeking company.

His laugh, his childlike spirit and his enthusiastic delight in learning and teaching about many of the classics in literature and music infected me. And while these traits were even more magnetic when we were smoking pot, they endured into the middle of the day when we were straight and stone-cold sober. Paul was Peter Pan, the Pied Piper, the promise of being forever young and eternally creative.

In a sense, Paul was also the first person who had acted as a mentor to me. He was too young to fully appreciate the emotional power and mental advantage this gave him, but he had figured out long before we met that he could use his charm to gain physical access to the opposite gender. He bragged, even to me, about the girl in his class he had screwed in the chapel at

Rome Catholic High when they were seniors. Rather than scaring me away, the tale created an allure, in part because of Paul's storytelling skills.

One afternoon, when I had stayed home pretending to be sick—something I had never done in earlier years—I asked Paul to come over to my house when my parents were both working at the store. He must have known that I was inviting him to end my virginity. Most young men would have simply pursued the obvious with vigor, but Paul brought with him a recording of Rimsky-Korsakov's *Scheherazade*. Other than the classical pieces I had learned as a piano student, or those my older sisters played before me, I was ignorant of classical music and had never before heard a symphony, live or recorded. Paul not only put the recording on the turntable for us to hear but he also told the story of the Prince and Princess from Scheherazade's *"1001 Arabian Nights."*

"A sorcerer consults the stars and signs," Paul said, "and realizes that Aladdin is the boy he needs. When they find a magic lamp and polish it, a genie appears and grants Aladdin three wishes." Paul spoke in a hushed and rapid tone, growing quicker and louder as the story went on. "Aladdin wishes for food and clothes first, but then he sees a beautiful Princess and asks the genie for the princess to fall in love with him, but the genie tells him he can't grant that wish,"

"Then Aladdin wishes to be wealthy, but somehow, the princess sees Aladdin's true wish and falls in love with him. But the evil sorcerer steals the lamp and makes the genie move the Princess and their palace to Africa. For years, Aladdin searches for the Princess; finally, he finds the evil sorcerer and the lamp, and defeats him. This time, he wishes only for the return of his Princess and the palace. And poof, his wish is granted. They live happily ever after and rule their kingdom wisely!"

And with that conclusion, the music swelled. Paul held me close and kissed me deeply, and I could only imagine that he was Aladdin and I was the Princess. We undressed each other, and, being a naïve virgin, it didn't matter to me then that the sex itself was not fully consummated. The turn-on was emotional and intellectual, the excitement in the story and the music.

To my parents, and eventually even to my old friend Marilyn, Paul came to represent a cult power under which I had allowed myself to fall. I began to mimic the tenor of his voice and repeat his sayings, "Far fucking out!" and "Bullshit is king." I became intrigued with folk music that Paul played for me, such as Hamilton Camp singing, "Pride of Man," and Walt Whitman became my favorite poet after we shared his verse.

Before meeting Paul, I had already begun to wear countercultural clothes. No longer interested in bourgeois tweeds and corduroy, I paid visits to the Salvation Army to buy cast-off army fatigues, faded blue denim bib overalls and work shirts. But after becoming involved with Paul, I wore them more often. To my mother, I was wearing the uniform of the devil, even though the garb was as American as the forces that fought in World War II and the farmers who labored in the Midwest.

Even more frightening to my mother and many of the priests and nuns at school, I began to read about Eastern religions such as Buddhism and Taoism. I sought to understand the Asian mind with which my country was at war. Gradually, I was no longer the same girl they had known and loved.

At some point during my senior year, I confided in Paul that I "hated" my father. This may have been partly due to the fact that my father hated Paul. While Paul did his best to be polite when he came to the door to pick me up, my father was cold and uninviting. The next day, the first thing my father would say to me was, "Why are you interested in a boy who grows his hair out like a girl? What's the matter with you? And what's the matter with him?"

To young men of the late 1960s and early 1970s, long hair was just a sign of the times, both an expression of love for music, peace and freedom and a sign of fear about the military draft. In another sign of the times, there was a game played by many of our high school's senior boys who "acted out" war in Vietnam. They would get drunk, go into the woods and pretend they were in combat, climbing into trees with BB guns to shoot at each other while, in reality, they waited to find out what number the local draft board had picked for them.

Among most older American adults, long hair in boys and men gave rise to disdain like that expressed by my father. In some families it may have been harmless banter between generations. But to my parents, Paul's long hair was a reason to feel hostile toward him, as it represented to them a lack of patriotism, an affinity for drug-crazed parties, and failure to embrace a productive work ethic. Their feelings toward Paul aggravated the increasing tension between me and my parents.

Furthermore, I suspect that as I grew into my later teen years, something about me reminded my mother of her older sister Leona. Understandably, this would have been a frightening feeling since my mother was only about ten years old when Leona had—in the throes of illness—threatened to kill her. Perhaps it was something about my eyes, or my dark hair, or the way I dressed that began to look scary to my mother.

What must have been worse for my mother was how I had grown increasingly alienated from and angry toward the dominant culture and "silent majority" politics that my parents represented and embraced. My mother gradually began to misinterpret this rift, shared by the majority of my generation, as a possible sign of mental illness.

My parents did not want to consider that I was consciously and purposely rejecting their values and beliefs. I'm sure it was easier to speculate that my choices might be the result of a terrible brain disorder over which I—and they—had no control. Mom and Dad cast my entire demeanor as one of withdrawal from normality, based on the very limited number of hours that I spent with them.

And yet, I was going to school and still obtaining grades that ranged from A minus to A, although they used to be A to A plus. I was cheerleading almost every day, even though my heart was no longer fully committed to the conformity of high school athletics and I was performing with the school chorus. At the same time, I worked with my good friend Barb on the creation of a special Halloween play at school featuring characters from the *Peanuts* comic strip engaged in some raw egg-throwing (with permission from the faculty). In short, my life at school was nearly as normal as ever.

I must admit however, that I had become edgy and rebellious against the most rigid of my teachers. I pleaded with Father Karlen, the school's designated guidance counselor, to be released from Physics in my senior year to enable me to take the only art course available at my school. Despite my long list of well-reasoned arguments, Father Karlen refused, insisting that anyone headed to college must take four years of science and in doing so, implying that art was only for those less capable.

I still went out at times with my old RCH friends, but my social circles were shifting toward those in Rome who were painted with the "hippie" brush. As this transition happened, what my parents saw in me was the result of my stepping aboard a ship that was sailing away from them. In that era, most older teenagers managed to keep that ship in port until they went away to college.

But I could not hold myself back any longer and began my experimentation while still living under my parents' roof. My mother's experience with her sister, and perhaps my father's experience with his baby sister, led them to see me as a stranger as I sailed away—a dangerous stranger who threatened their way of life, and who might one day attack even their physical lives.

By the summer of 1969, my faith further shattered by my break with Tom, I began "acting out" like throngs of young people in the U.S. were doing at the time. By August, I had changed from a devout, obedient Catholic girl who aced every test and displayed happy energetic school spirit to someone entirely different. I dabbled in pot and hallucinogens, experimented with sex, and allowed my nagging doubts about the virgin birth and divinity of Jesus to be overwhelmed by agnosticism.

By the fall of my senior year in high school, I had developed a generalized anger toward the TV, which had replaced direct family conversation and human interaction in our household, as it had in many others. One night in particular, my anger toward both my father and television boiled over. That morning my father had given me his usual sloppy neck kiss and later that day at school, I had an argument over Vietnam with a classmate. Before dinner, my father was berating my mother over something she had done at the store that day. As tensions within me were boiling, during dinner, I tried to talk with my parents about my college plans, but my father kept telling me to be quiet so he could hear a TV newsman say what was wrong with my generation.

At that point, I slammed my fork down on my plate, got up, walked around the table and kicked the TV set. Without turning back, I ran to my room and slammed the door.

After the clatter from kitchen clean-up ended, my mother came to my room and knocked lightly, and I opened the door.

"What's wrong Lin? What's bothering you?"

"Can't you tell what's wrong?" I asked incredulously. "Everything is wrong."

I raised my voice, and even though my mother was not the real source of my anger, she had come to represent what was wrong. Everything that culminated within me led me to see her as the problem, from her quiet acceptance of my father's behavior, to the silence of the Church about the injustice of the Vietnam War, to the constant harping about how terrible young people had become. The girl inside me who had once done her best to cheer up my mother, to give her an affectionate pat on the butt when she leaned over to get something out of the oven, or to help her in the kitchen while her husband criticized her relentlessly–that girl now shut her out.

"I just want to be left alone," I said.

And like the quiet, shy and obedient soul she was, my mother left me alone in my bedroom.

After writing in my diary about my feelings and explorations, I did what most adolescents will do in their forgetfulness. Giving no thought to the possible consequences, I left the diary out where my parents could easily find and read it. And read it they would.

DECEMBER 1969 IN CONTEXT

Oh, a storm is threat'ning my very life today
If I don't get some shelter, Oh yeah, I'm gonna fade away...

— "Gimme Shelter"
The Rolling Stones 1969

FOLLOWING A VISIT FROM MARILYN, MY old East Syracuse friend, during Thanksgiving break when she spent time with me, Paul and some of our other friends, she wrote me a long, candid letter. Among other things, she told me I was not being true to myself, that I was allowing Paul to control me, and that my behavior was robotic. Given our long-term friendship and my trust in Marilyn, I took her letter very seriously, and began to see that I needed to reestablish my own sense of self. Unfortunately, this realization came a bit late.

It was now Christmas vacation, just two months after my 17th birthday and before any of my siblings had arrived to celebrate the holidays. I didn't notice that it was a Saturday at 9 AM and my father had not yet left home for the store, though he was usually gone by 7 AM. My mother walked into my bedroom and asked me to come to the dining room. "Your father and I have something we want to talk to you about," she said. I could hear from the tone of her voice that it was not going to be good—that they weren't going to ask me what I wanted for Christmas, or where I wanted to go to college next fall.

I had already braced myself for a difficult encounter before Mom led me to the dining room, where my father was seated at his usual "head of the table" seat, and my mother at the other end. When I looked down and saw my diary on the table in front of her, my heart started to race, my face grew hot and my legs seemed paralyzed.

"Sit down," my father said.

I managed to move my body to a sitting position, on the side of the table facing the window. I stared at the outdoors in front of me, searching for a way to escape. Then my mother began as she picked up my diary.

"You left this out on your dresser and we are very concerned about what's in it."

Quickly I turned my head toward her and glared. "How could you read my diary? It's mine, it's private! You wouldn't understand what's in it at all."

My father interjected, "Oh, I think we can understand some of it."

I did everything I could to control myself. This included grasping the sides of the seat on the chair beneath me and not moving one muscle at the risk that I would pick something up and throw it at the window or the wall. I thought about the entries in my diary describing in detail what it felt like to smoke pot for the first time or how I had finally lost my virginity. I also knew that my efforts to evoke a muse to write poetry and to open my mind to new vistas in my diary would appear to my mother and father as incoherent scrawls.

"We don't understand what's been happening to you. We're afraid you're doing things where you'll end up hurting yourself, so we went to talk to the guidance office at school for help."

In other words, I thought, they did not come to me first to discuss my diary entries and ask me questions about what was there or suggest that I go with them to the guidance office. They did not talk to me at all until now.

The principal of Rome Catholic High School was a conservative Papist and a former Marine chaplain, and the guidance officer was another former military man. Here I was an opponent of the Vietnam War who had openly questioned Catholic doctrine about guardian angels in my daily religion class. In recent months, I had grown curious about why Catholicism had banned witchcraft and I had taken out books from the public library that told a side of history I'd never heard at school, such as how Saint Thomas More was known for burning heretics at the stake. My parents had turned to this school of thought for advice about how to deal with behavior that they had never seen before in any of their older children.

"Father Morelle gave us the name of a doctor and we went to see him," she continued.

"What kind of doctor?"

"He's a psychiatrist who has a lot of experience. He takes care of the nuns when they need counseling. The doctor said he has reason to believe you've been using drugs that are laced with some damaging chemicals, and he gave us a prescription for medicine that will counter the effects of these bad drugs."

"Why does he think that? He hasn't talked to me, he hasn't even seen me," I protested, my voice rising, my heart pounding. "How can he prescribe medicine for a patient he hasn't even met?" I had heard that some street drugs could be "cut with shit" and you needed to be careful. But how did this doctor have any idea what drugs I had taken?

"We showed him your diary," my mother answered. "He said he knows what kind of drugs have been circulating around here. You need to start taking this medicine to avoid the damage from the drugs you've taken."

My mother handed me a large brown vial of prescription medicine. I looked at the label–"Trilafon." I didn't know what it was but I knew that if I refused to take it, I could end up like my friend's mother who was sent for electroshock therapy at Marcy State when she refused to take her meds. By the age of 17 in the era of civil rights battles, anti-war protests and political assassinations, I had learned that the punishment only gets more severe for those who don't cooperate.

The pills were round, with a hard, shiny gray coating, and I was told to take two pills, four times per day. If current pharmaceutical images show what Trilafon looked like in 1970, it confirms my recollection that I was taking 64 milligrams of the drug per day. I quickly discovered through firsthand experience that Trilafon acts like a chemical lobotomy, turning active human minds into catatonic bumps on a log.

Decades later, I learned through research that Trilafon is a powerful anti-psychotic drug in the Thorazine family, with the generic name perphenazine, and that the dosage on the bottle that my mother handed to me is now considered the absolute maximum dosage, even for an adult who is a truly raving, hospitalized schizophrenic. At that dosage, even a hospitalized adult should be kept under constant monitoring for adverse effects, one of the most common of which is the development of uncontrollable muscular symptoms like those of Parkinson's Disease.

Perphenazine or Trilafon is not recommended at all for children 12 and under, and the lowest possible adult dosage is recommended for hospitalized children above age 12.[40]

* * * *

"The people have become deluded into thinking there's a cure for everything if you have enough money," claimed Dr. Anthony Sainz, research director at nearby Marcy State Hospital. "Research, thus, has become more difficult," Dr. Sainz said. "It is like asking a doctor to cure you but don't diagnose what's the matter with you."[41]

Utica Daily Press, October 5, 1966

INTRODUCING TRILAFON (PERPHENAZINE)

MOST READERS MAY WANT TO SKIP this chapter. Editors may think it should be summarized or heavily edited. But that in essence is the problem for people who are prescribed drugs like these; we ignore the warnings, the side effects and the risks. We skip over the fine print. Supposedly intended to "treat" people who are diagnosed with some mental condition or illness, psychotropic drugs often create other problems. They can lead to permanent damage to the brain or other organs.

With that being said, I include the full information on Trilafon (perphenazine) from Drug Information Online, as published in October 2012.[42] This was the drug I was given a hefty dose of over a period of about two years between the ages of 17 and 19. It was not possible for me to skip over the fine print.

Trilafon became a major character in my story, and this chapter explains why.

TRILAFON-Generic Name: perphenazine (per-FEN-a-zeen)
For the Consumer

What is Trilafon (perphenazine)?

Perphenazine is an anti-psychotic medication in a group of drugs called phenothiazines (FEEN-oh-THYE-a-zeens). It works by changing the actions of chemicals in your brain.

Perphenazine is used to treat psychotic disorders such as schizophrenia. It is also used to control severe nausea and vomiting.

Perphenazine may also be used for purposes not listed in this medication guide.

What is the most important information I should know about Trilafon (perphenazine)?

Stop using this medication and call your doctor at once if you have twitching or uncontrollable movements of your eyes, lips, tongue, face, arms, or legs. These could be early signs of dangerous side effects. Perphenazine is not for use in psychotic conditions related to dementia. Perphenazine may cause heart failure, sudden death, or pneumonia in older adults with dementia-related conditions. Do not use perphenazine if you have liver disease, brain damage, bone marrow depression, a blood cell disorder, or if you are also using large amounts of alcohol or medicines that make you sleepy. Do not use if you are allergic to perphenazine or other phenothiazines.

Before you take perphenazine, tell your doctor if you have severe depression, heart disease or high blood pressure, liver or kidney disease, severe asthma or breathing problems, history of seizures, Parkinson's disease, past or present breast cancer, adrenal gland tumor, enlarged prostate or urination problems, glaucoma, low levels of calcium in your blood, or if you have ever had serious side effects while using chlorpromazine or similar medicines.

Before taking perphenazine, tell your doctor about all other medications you use.

For Health Professionals

Pharmacology: Effects apparently caused by postsynaptic dopamine receptor blockade in CNS (Central Nervous System)

WARNINGS

Increased Mortality in Elderly Patients with Dementia-Related Psychosis

Elderly patients with dementia-related psychosis treated with antipsychotic drugs are at an increased risk of death. Perphenazine is not approved for the treatment of patients with dementia-related psychosis (see BOXED WARNING).

Tardive dyskinesia, a syndrome consisting of potentially irreversible, involuntary, dyskinetic movements, may develop in patients treated with antipsychotic drugs. Older patients are at increased risk for development of tardive dyskinesia. Although the prevalence of the syndrome appears to be highest among the elderly, especially elderly women, it is impossible to rely upon prevalence estimates to predict, at the inception of antipsychotic treatment, which patients are likely to develop the syndrome. Whether antipsychotic drug products differ in their potential to cause tardive dyskinesia is unknown.

Both the risk of developing the syndrome and the likelihood that it will become irreversible are believed to increase as the duration of treatment and the total cumulative dose of antipsychotic drugs administered to the patient increase. However, the syndrome can develop, although much less commonly, after relatively brief treatment periods at low doses.

There is no known treatment for established cases of tardive dyskinesia, although the syndrome may remit, partially or completely, if antipsychotic treatment is withdrawn. Antipsychotic treatment itself, however, may suppress (or partially suppress) the signs and symptoms of the syndrome, and thereby may possibly mask the underlying disease process. The effect that symptomatic suppression has upon the long-term course of the syndrome is unknown.

Given these considerations, especially in the elderly, antipsychotics should be prescribed in a manner that is most likely to minimize the occurrence of tardive dyskinesia. Chronic antipsychotic treatment should generally be reserved for patients who suffer from a chronic illness that 1) is known to respond to antipsychotic drugs, and 2) for whom alternative, equally effective, but potentially less harmful treatments are not available or appropriate. In patients who do require chronic treatment, the smallest dose and the shortest duration of treatment producing a satisfactory clinical response should be sought. The need for continued treatment should be reassessed periodically.

If signs and symptoms of tardive dyskinesia appear in a patient on antipsychotics, drug discontinuation should be considered. However, some patients may require treatment despite the presence of the syndrome. (For further information about the description of tardive dyskinesia and its clinical detection, please refer to Information for Patients and ADVERSE REACTIONS).

Neuroleptic Malignant Syndrome (NMS)

A potentially fatal symptom complex, sometimes referred to as Neuroleptic Malignant Syndrome (NMS), has been reported in association with antipsychotic drugs. Clinical manifestations of NMS are hyperpyrexia, muscle rigidity, altered mental status and evidence of autonomic instability (irregular pulse or blood pressure, tachycardia, diaphoresis, and cardiac dysrhythmias).

The diagnostic evaluation of patients with this syndrome is complicated. In arriving at a diagnosis, it is important to identify cases where the clinical presentation includes both serious medical illness (e.g., pneumonia, systemic infection, etc.) and untreated or inadequately treated extrapyramidal signs and symptoms (EPS). Other important considerations in the differential diagnosis include central anticholinergic toxicity, heat stroke, drug fever and primary central nervous system (CNS) pathology.

The management of NMS should include 1) immediate discontinuation of antipsychotic drugs and other drugs not essential to concurrent therapy, 2) intensive symptomatic treatment and medical monitoring, and 3) treatment of any concomitant serious medical problems for which specific treatments are available. There is no general agreement about specific pharmacological treatment regimens for uncomplicated NMS.

If a patient requires antipsychotic drug treatment after recovery from NMS, the reintroduction of drug therapy should be carefully considered. The patient should be carefully monitored, since recurrences of NMS have been reported.

If hypotension develops, epinephrine should not be administered since its action is blocked and partially reversed by Perphenazine. If a vasopressor is needed, norepinephrine may be used. Severe, acute hypotension has occurred with the use of phenothiazines and is particularly likely to occur in patients with mitral insufficiency or pheochromocytoma. Rebound hypertension may occur in pheochromocytoma patients.

Perphenazine products can lower the convulsive threshold in susceptible individuals; they should be used with caution in alcohol withdrawal and in patients with convulsive disorders. If the patient is being treated with an anticonvulsant agent, increased dosage of that agent may be required when Perphenazine products are used concomitantly.

Perphenazine products should be used with caution in patients with psychic depression.

Perphenazine may impair the mental and/or physical abilities required for the performance of hazardous tasks such as driving a car or operating machinery; therefore, the patient should be warned accordingly.

Perphenazine products are not recommended for pediatric patients under 12 years of age.

Leukopenia, Neutropenia and Agranulocytosis

In clinical trial and post-marketing experience, events of leukopenia/neutropenia have been reported temporally related to antipsychotic agents, including Perphenazine Tablets, USP. Agranulocytosis (including fatal cases) has also been reported. Possible risk factors for leukopenia/neutropenia include pre-existing low white blood cell count (WBC) and history of drug induced leukopenia/neutropenia. Patients with a pre-existing low WBC or a history of drug induced leukopenia/neutropenia should have their complete blood count (CBC) monitored frequently during the first few months of therapy and should discontinue Perphenazine Tablets, USP at the first sign of a decline in WBC in the absence of other causative factors.

Patients with neutropenia should be carefully monitored for fever or other symptoms or signs of infection and treated promptly if such symptoms or signs occur. Patients with severe neutropenia (absolute neutrophil count <1000/mm3) should discontinue Perphenazine Tablets, USP and have their WBC followed until recovery.

For more information, see

http://www.drugs.com/pro/perphenazine.html

Perphenazine Side Effects
For the Professional

Perphenazine

Not all of the following adverse reactions have been reported with this specific drug; however, pharmacological similarities among various phenothiazine derivatives require that each be considered. With the piperazine group (of which Perphenazine is an example), the extrapyramidal symptoms are more common, and others (e.g., sedative effects, jaundice, and blood dyscrasias) are less frequently seen.

CNS Effects

Extrapyramidal Reactions: opisthotonus, trismus, torticollis, retrocollis, aching and numbness of the limbs, motor restlessness, oculogyric crisis, hyperreflexia, dystonia, including protrusion, discoloration, aching and rounding of the tongue, tonic spasm of the masticatory muscles, tight feeling in the throat, slurred speech, dysphagia, akathisia, dyskinesia, parkinsonism, and ataxia. Their incidence and severity usually increase with an increase in dosage, but there is considerable individual variation in the tendency to develop such symptoms. Extrapyramidal symptoms can usually be controlled by the concomitant use of effective antiparkinsonian drugs, such as benztropine mesylate, and/or by reduction in dosage. In some instances, however, these extrapyramidal reactions may persist after discontinuation of treatment with Perphenazine.

Persistent Tardive Dyskinesia: As with all antipsychotic agents, tardive dyskinesia may appear in some patients on long-term therapy or may appear after drug therapy has been discontinued. Although the risk appears to be greater in elderly patients on high-dose therapy, especially females, it may occur in either sex and in children. The symptoms are persistent and in some patients appear to be irreversible. The syndrome is characterized by rhythmical, involuntary movements of the tongue, face, mouth or jaw (e.g., protrusion of tongue, puffing of cheeks, puckering of mouth, chewing movements). Sometimes these may be accompanied by involuntary movements of the extremities. There is no known effective treatment for tardive dyskinesia; antiparkinsonism agents usually do not alleviate the symptoms of this syndrome. It is suggested that all antipsychotic agents be discontinued if these symptoms appear. Should it be necessary to reinstitute treatment, or increase the dosage of the agent, or switch to a different antipsychotic agent, the syndrome may be masked. It has been reported that fine, vermicular movements of the tongue may be an early sign of the syndrome, and if the medication is stopped at that time the syndrome may not develop.

Other CNS Effects: include cerebral edema; abnormality of cerebrospinal fluid proteins; convulsive seizures, particularly in patients with EEG abnormalities or a history of such disorders; and headaches.

Neuroleptic malignant syndrome has been reported in patients treated with antipsychotic drugs.

Drowsiness may occur, particularly during the first or second week, after which it generally disappears. If troublesome, lower the dosage. Hypnotic effects appear to be minimal, especially in patients who are permitted to remain active.

Adverse behavioral effects include paradoxical exacerbation of psychotic symptoms, catatonic-like states, paranoid reactions, lethargy, paradoxical excitement, restlessness, hyperactivity, nocturnal confusion, bizarre dreams, and insomnia.

Hyperreflexia has been reported in the newborn when a phenothiazine was used during pregnancy.

Autonomic Effects: dry mouth or salivation, nausea, vomiting, diarrhea, anorexia, constipation, obstipation, fecal impaction, urinary retention, frequency or incontinence, bladder paralysis, polyuria, nasal congestion, pallor, myosis, mydriasis, blurred vision, glaucoma, perspiration, hypertension, hypotension, and change in pulse rate occasionally may occur. Significant autonomic effects have been infrequent in patients receiving less than 24 mg Perphenazine daily.

Adynamic ileus occasionally occurs with phenothiazine therapy, and if severe, can result in complications and death. It is of particular concern in psychiatric patients, who may fail to seek treatment of the condition.

Allergic Effects: urticaria, erythema, eczema, exfoliative dermatitis, pruritus, photosensitivity, asthma, fever, anaphylactoid reactions, laryngeal edema, and angioneurotic edema; contact dermatitis in nursing personnel administering the drug; and in extremely rare instances, individual idiosyncrasy or hypersensitivity to phenothiazines has resulted in cerebral edema, circulatory collapse, and death.

Endocrine Effects: lactation, galactorrhea, moderate breast enlargement in females and gynecomastia in males on large doses, disturbances in the menstrual cycle, amenorrhea, changes in libido, inhibition of ejaculation, syndrome of inappropriate ADH (antidiuretic hormone) secretion, false positive pregnancy tests, hyperglycemia, hypoglycemia, glycosuria.

Cardiovascular Effects: postural hypotension, tachycardia (especially with sudden marked increase in dosage), bradycardia, cardiac arrest, faintness, and dizziness. Occasionally the hypotensive effect may produce a shock-like condition. ECG changes, nonspecific (quinidine-like effect) usually reversible, have been observed in some patients receiving phenothiazine antipsychotics.

Sudden death has occasionally been reported in patients who have received phenothiazines. In some cases, the death was apparently due to cardiac arrest; in others, the cause appeared to be asphyxia due to failure of the cough reflex. In some patients, the cause could not be determined nor could it be established that the death was due to the phenothiazine.

Hematological Effects: agranulocytosis, eosinophilia, leukopenia, hemolytic anemia, thrombocytopenic purpura, and pancytopenia. Most cases of agranulocytosis have occurred between the fourth and tenth weeks of therapy. Patients should be watched closely, especially during that period, for the sudden appearance of sore throat or signs of infection. If white blood cell and differential cell counts show significant cellular depression, discontinue the drug and start appropriate therapy. However, a slightly lowered white count is not in itself an indication to discontinue the drug.

Other Effects: Special considerations in long-term therapy include pigmentation of the skin, occurring chiefly in the exposed areas; ocular changes consisting of deposition of fine particulate matter in the cornea and lens, progressing in more severe cases to star-shaped lenticular opacities; epithelial keratopathies; and pigmentary retinopathy. Also noted: peripheral edema, reversed epinephrine effect, increase in PBI not attributable to an increase in thyroxine, parotid swelling (rare), hyperpyrexia, systemic lupus erythematosus-like syndrome, increases in appetite and weight, polyphagia, photophobia, and muscle weakness.

Liver damage (biliary stasis) may occur. Jaundice may occur, usually between the second and fourth weeks of treatment, and is regarded as a hypersensitivity reaction. Incidence is low. The clinical picture resembles infectious hepatitis but with laboratory features of obstructive jaundice. It is usually reversible; however, chronic jaundice has been reported.

Adverse Reactions

Cardiovascular: Orthostatic hypotension; hypertension; tachycardia; bradycardia; syncope; cardiac arrest; circulatory collapse; ECG changes.

CNS: Lightheadedness; faintness; dizziness; pseudoparkinsonism; dystonia; dyskinesia, motor restlessness; oculogyric crisis; dystonias; hyperreflexia; tardive dyskinesia; drowsiness; headache; fatigue; abnormalities of the cerebrospinal fluid proteins; paradoxical excitement or exacerbation of psychotic symptoms; catatonic-like states; weakness; tremor; paranoid reactions; lethargy; seizures; hyperactivity; nocturnal confusion; bizarre dreams; vertigo; insomnia.

Dermatologic: Photosensitivity; skin pigmentation; dry skin; exfoliative dermatitis; urticarial rash; maculopapular hypersensitivity reaction; seborrhea; eczema; pruritus.

EENT: Pigmentary retinopathy; glaucoma; photophobia; blurred vision; mydriasis; increased IOP; dry mouth or throat; nasal congestion.

GI: Dyspepsia; adynamic ileus (may result in death); nausea; vomiting; constipation.

Genitourinary: Breast enlargement; galactorrhea; urinary hesitancy or retention; impotence; sexual dysfunction; menstrual irregularities.

Hematologic: Agranulocytosis; eosinophilia; leukopenia; hemolytic anemia; thrombocytopenic purpura; pancytopenia.

Hepatic: Jaundice.

Metabolic: Hyperglycemia; hypoglycemia; decreased cholesterol.

Respiratory: Laryngospasm; bronchospasm; dyspnea.

Miscellaneous: Increases in appetite and weight; polydipsia; increased prolactin levels.[43]

Tragic images of injured and killed children, women and men were broadcast nightly into American living rooms during the Vietnam War, fueling anti-war sentiment. Photo by P.J. Griffith, reprinted with permission of Magnum Photos, Inc. For more information on Vietnam photos by Griffith, see: http://www.magnumphotos.com

Linda, summer of 1969, cropped from a group photo of friends on a car in a wooded area outside Rome, NY.

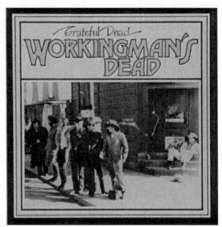

Music of the late 1960s was a powerful
presence in a rising youth counterculture.

VI

LOCKED UP

LOCKED UP

I TOLD ANNE AND PAUL WHAT was happening, though my parents had insisted that I stop seeing or talking to them. Claiming I was going to Chris' house, I'd go down the street to Anne's instead and when I saw Paul there, I could already tell I was changing. I felt like a zombie: I could not laugh, smile, cry, or change the tenor of my voice. In psychological terms, my affect was as flat as the surface of a Texas highway.

"Look, here's the pill," I said to Paul. These were the days long before Internet search engines. "It's called Trilafon. Can you find out what it is? It's making me feel like a nothing. My parents told me not to see you. I don't know what to do."

"I'm sorry Linda, I'm in trouble now, too," Paul replied. "They're sending me back to school. Anyway, you should stay away from me."

As with Tom the previous summer, the boy I loved was walking away and leaving me alone and in pain. At the end of the holiday break not too long after, both Paul and Anne went back to college. A renewed sense of abandonment surged through my veins, compounded by the effect of the drug and the fact that my parents had so easily agreed to prescribe it. While my hands were free, I might as well have been in a straightjacket, because I could barely move.

After taking the medication for several weeks during and after Christmas vacation, my parents sat down with me once again in the dining room. It was a Saturday and I was supposed to go back to school the following week.

"The doctor says that it would be best if you were in the hospital now, since they need to monitor the effect of the medication," said my mother. "The medication can affect your school work temporarily, so it's best if you don't go to school right now. St. Elizabeth's Hospital in Utica can take you in today. You need to pack some clothes."

I had read Ken Kesey's *One Flew Over the Cuckoo's Nest*, and understood what could happen when someone is committed to a psychiatric ward. In those years, it was considered a badge of political courage in some circles to be sent away against your will. I also knew it was common for creative, countercultural people in all eras to be considered somewhat crazy.

But here were my parents, my own mom and dad, telling me I had to go away. What kind of threat did they think I was?

I went to my room, opened my closet and drawers and tried to choose what to take to the hospital. Sweatpants and t-shirt? Blue jeans and peasant blouse? But even the smallest choice seemed like an insurmountable decision. My mind felt literally torn. My mom and dad had suddenly decided that whatever I said or thought was suspect, and whatever this doctor said was gospel truth, even though the doctor hadn't even met me yet. From my end, I was totally confused. I no longer knew whether or not I could believe or trust what my parents were telling me. Even worse, I was no longer sure I could trust myself.

In the past, even when times were rough, I always had the holidays to enjoy. I'm sure I received some gifts for Christmas in 1969, but I have no recollection of anything related to the holiday that year. I only remember the bottle of pills, the thick curtain that this so-called medicine pulled down between the rest of the world and me. This was only compounded by the shock that I was being punished so harshly when my behavior seemed so typical of people my age in those years.

It seems that Dr. Sainz had confirmed my mother's worst fears when he delivered his diagnosis before seeing me, based only on her description of my behavior and a glance through my diary. He told her that I was probably schizophrenic, just as her sister Leona had probably been. She readily accepted this "diagnosis"—her daughter had a disorder that would require, or perhaps allow, her and my father to relinquish all responsibility for my feelings, thoughts and deeds and turn me over to the care of a strange doctor and even stranger chemicals. At the time, my mother told my sister Diane that she would rather see me have cancer than to be sick the way her sister Leona had been. My father stood by silently, perhaps recalling his own past losses of a mother and then a baby sister.

When I arrived at the hospital, I didn't need to read the signs on the walls to know that I was in the psychiatric ward. It became crystal clear when I sat in the patient lounge area and witnessed the behavior of other patients. There was Charlie, who spent hours shuffling cards, laying them out for solitaire, and then picking them up again without ever playing the hand he had dealt himself. Then there was Katharine, a lovely young woman about two years older than me. I tried to hang around with her and joke about being considered crazy, but she said, "No, I really am sick. I really hear voices and see things that aren't there."

Since I had never experienced hallucinations like Katharine's, I didn't feel I could share with her what was happening to me. To me, *acting* crazy had just been a childish joke; an aesthetic and political trick that I could turn on and off. That is, until I landed in a psychiatric ward.

I was given a room with two beds, but I was the only person in the room. I had brought with me Thomas Merton's *The Seven Storey Mountain*, which I had begun reading about a month earlier. I also had Walt Whitman's *Leaves of Grass*, which I usually read every day.

At this point, I had been taking the medication for three or four weeks and had been in the hospital for three days, but I still had not met the doctor who put me there. During the first few days, I had visits from my parents, my friend Marilyn and my favorite teacher, Father Stephan, who all had little to say as they stood with tears in their eyes. Seeing Father Stephan reminded me what would be happening soon with the rest of my senior class, while I was in the hospital.

In those years, high-school students took the national merit scholarship exam in the second semester of their senior year. This meant I was just weeks away from the test that could determine whether or not I could attend the college I most preferred—Cornell University. Given my grades and Regents exam scores for the previous three-and-a-half years, I was on my way to becoming the valedictorian of my high school class. Before I was locked away, I'd been in a contest with a high-IQ male student named Larry who was viewed as a "coaster" since he relied more on his photographic memory than on hard work. Father Stephan had devised a bet to spur Larry's competitive instincts, saying he'd give him $100 if he became the valedictorian.

My competitiveness was crippled. Just weeks away from this important test, by the fourth day I had spent in the hospital, my eyesight had begun to fail. When I tried to read, the lines on the page quadrupled and blurred. Within another day, my small

17-year-old breasts, which had little sexual experience and certainly no experience with pregnancy, were oozing milk.

The following day, I finally had an appointment with the doctor.

A nurse led me into an office and asked me to sit down. About five minutes later, the door opened and a tall man with graying dark hair and glasses entered the room. I was shocked to see that this was the same man who had addressed me and other junior leaders in Syracuse the year before. The very same man who had rambled in a way that seemed incoherent to us about drunken animals in the jungle in thickly accented speech.

"Hello, I'm Doctor Sainz," he said with a large smile, and the same accent I remembered.

"I've met you before," I said.

"Oh? And where was that?" The look of disbelief in his eyes and the condescending tone of his voice made me realize that he assumed whatever I said was a delusion.

"You spoke to a group of junior leaders in Syracuse. You were talking about animals in the jungle who got drunk from fermented fruit juice," I recalled. While I tried as hard as I could to keep a straight face, this memory made the corner of my mouth curl, and I feared it gave away the fact that I already considered him a ridiculous buffoon. On top of everything else, this was not a good beginning to what was allegedly a therapeutic relationship.

When he asked how I was feeling, I told him that my breasts were producing milk, and that my vision was so blurry that I was unable to read. The doctor listened and said, "We'll adjust the medication." Then he got up, adding as he showed me to the door, "It's been good to meet you. I'll see you again in a few days."

The next day, I was on a slightly lower dose of Trilafon and a new drug—Ritalin.

ENTER: RITALIN

Since the days I took Ritalin, it has become one of the primary drugs prescribed for children diagnosed with ADD (attention deficit disorder). I am not sure what rationale Doctor Sainz had in mind when he added it to my regimen, other than experimentation.

Once again, readers may choose to skip this detail. However, I believe that it is time for us all to read the fine print about the pharmaceuticals we are feeding to so many of our children. This description of Ritalin comes from Drug Information Online, updated October 2012.

RITALIN - Generic Name: methylphenidate (oral) (METH-il-FEN-i-date)

For the consumer:

What is Ritalin?

Ritalin (methylphenidate) is a central nervous system stimulant. It affects chemicals in the brain and nerves that contribute to hyperactivity and impulse control.

Ritalin is used to treat attention deficit disorder (ADD) and attention deficit hyperactivity disorder (ADHD). Ritalin is also used in the treatment of a sleep disorder called narcolepsy (an uncontrollable desire to sleep). When given for attention deficit disorders, Ritalin should be an integral part of a total treatment program that may include counseling or other therapies.

Ritalin may also be used for purposes not listed in this medication guide.

Important information about Ritalin

Do not use Ritalin if you have used an MAO inhibitor such as furazolidone (Furoxone), isocarboxazid (Marplan), phenelzine (Nardil), rasagiline (Azilect), selegiline (Eldepryl, Emsam), or tranylcypromine (Parnate) within the past 14 days. Serious, life-threatening side effects can occur if you use Ritalin before the MAO inhibitor has cleared from your body. Do not use this medication if you are allergic to Ritalin or if you have glaucoma, overactive thyroid, severe high blood pressure, tics or Tourette's syndrome, angina, heart failure, heart rhythm disorder, recent heart attack, a hereditary condition such as fructose intolerance, glucose-galactose malabsorption, or sucrase-isomaltase deficiency, or severe anxiety, tension, or agitation.

Ritalin may be habit-forming and should be used only by the person it was prescribed for. Never share Ritalin with another person, especially someone with a history of drug abuse or addiction. Keep the medication in a place where others cannot get to it.

For Health Professionals:

Methylphenidate Hydrochloride. Pronunciation: (meth-il-FEN-i-date HYE-droe-KLOR-ide)

Class: CNS stimulant

Pharmacology: Exact mechanism of action unknown, but presumably activates brain stem cell arousal system and cortex to produce its stimulant effect. Methylphenidate is thought to block reuptake of norepinephrine and dopamine into the presynaptic neuron and increase release of these monoamines into extraneuronal space.

Warnings: Use with caution in emotionally unstable patients, such as those with a history of alcoholism or drug dependence, because such patients may increase dosage on their own initiative. Chronically abusive use can lead to marked tolerance and psychic dependence with varying degrees of abnormal behavior. Frank psychotic episodes can occur, especially with parenteral use. Careful supervision is needed during drug withdrawal because severe depression and the effects of chronic over activity can be unmasked. Long-term follow-up may be needed because of the patient's basic personality disturbances.

Indications and Usage: Treatment of attention deficit disorder (ADD)/attention deficit hyperactivity disorder (ADHD); narcolepsy (except Concerta, Daytrana, Metadate CD, Ritalin LA).

Unlabeled Uses: Depression in medically ill elderly patients; alleviation of neurobehavioral symptoms after traumatic brain injury; improvement in pain control, sedation, or both in patients receiving opiates.

Contraindications: Marked anxiety, agitation, and tension; glaucoma; motor tics; family history or diagnosis of Tourette syndrome; concurrent treatment with MAOIs and within a minimum of 14 days following discontinuation of an MAOI; hypersensitivity to methylphenidate or other components of the products; severe hypertension; angina pectoris; cardiac arrhythmias; heart failure; recent MI; hyperthyroidism or thyrotoxicosis.

Adverse Reactions

Cardiovascular: Cardiac arrhythmias; cerebral arteritis and/or occlusion; changes in pulse and BP; tachycardia (5%); palpitations (3%); angina pectoris, bradycardia, cardiac arrest, extrasystoles, Raynaud phenomenon, supraventricular tachycardia, ventricular extrasystoles (postmarketing).

CNS: Headache (22%); insomnia (12%); anxiety (8%); dizziness (7%); irritability (6%); depressed mood (4%); nervousness, restlessness, tremor (3%); aggression, agitation, decreased libido, depression, teeth grinding, vertigo (2%); affect lability, confusional state, paresthesia, sedation, tension, tension headache (1%); drowsiness; dyskinesia; NMS; toxic psychosis; abnormal behavior, auditory hallucinations, convulsions, disorientation, dyskinesia, grand mal convulsions, hallucinations, hyperactivity, mania, reversible ischemic neurologic deficit, suicidal behavior including suicide, visual hallucinations (postmarketing).

Transdermal: Insomnia (30%); headache (28%); tic (7%); affect lability (6%).

Dermatologic: Alopecia, erythema, erythema multiforme, exfoliative dermatitis, fixed drug eruption, itching, purpura, rash, urticaria; bullous conditions, eruptions, exanthemas, pruritus (postmarketing).

Transdermal: Erythema.

EENT: Nasopharyngitis (3%); pharyngolaryngeal pain (2%); diplopia, mydriasis, visual disturbances (postmarketing).

Transdermal: Nasal congestion (6%); nasopharyngitis (5%).

GI: Dry mouth (14%); nausea (13%); upper abdominal pain (6%); vomiting (3%); dyspepsia (2%); constipation (1%); abdominal pain.

Transdermal: Nausea (12%); vomiting (10%).

Hematologic-Lymphatic: Anemia and/or leukopenia; pancytopenia, thrombocytopenia, thrombocytopenic purpura (postmarketing).

Hepatic: Abnormal liver function.

Hypersensitivity: Hypersensitivity reactions including anaphylactic reactions, angioedema, auricular swelling, bullous conditions, exfoliative conditions (postmarketing).

Lab Tests: Abnormal WBC count, decreased platelet count, increased bilirubin, increased blood alkaline phosphatase, increased hepatic enzymes (postmarketing).

Metabolic-Nutritional: Decreased appetite (25%); decreased weight (7%); anorexia (2%).

Transdermal: Anorexia (46%); decreased appetite (26%).

Musculoskeletal: Muscle tightness (2%); arthralgia, muscle twitching, myalgia (postmarketing).

Respiratory: Cough, upper respiratory tract infection (2%).

Miscellaneous: Hyperhidrosis (5%); fever (3%); hyperpyrexia (2%); Tourette syndrome; chest discomfort, chest pain, decreased drug effects, decreased therapeutic response, peripheral coldness, sudden death (postmarketing).

Transdermal: Viral infection (28%).[44]

WHO IS THIS DOCTOR?

AFTER ONE MORE WEEK IN THE hospital and the adjusted dosage, the milk gradually stopped flowing and my vision problems were replaced by a physical and mental restlessness. Interfering with my ability to sit still with a book in front of me, I began to roam around the hospital ward with my only friend, Katharine, or sit with my fellow inmates. I would try to get them to play checkers with me instead of obsessively counting or begging everyone who passed nearby for cigarettes or talking about aliens and spaceships.

Father Stephan came to visit me again and he did his best to assure me that I would be out of the hospital and OK soon. But it was obvious from the look on his face that it upset him to see my condition and environment, and that he did not fully believe the words he was expressing to me. Nevertheless, the fact that he took the time to see me and express caring concern in person—the only one of my teachers to do so—gave me some comfort that I was not completely cut off from the rest of the world.

After about two weeks, I was finally released from the hospital and soon after, I started back at school. As a caveat of my "treatment," I had to attend an hour-long weekly session with Dr. Sainz in his Rome office and continue taking the medication.

I doubt that my parents knew anything about this doctor, except that the principal of Rome Catholic High School had recommended him. To reach closure on my experience as his patient, it became essential that I discover more about him.

With the advent of online search engines, including archived psychiatric journals and searchable historic newspaper content through sites like Fulton History, a database of New York State historical newspapers, or Newspaper Archives, a similar database for news articles and events, I was able to piece together his history.[45]

Over a period of several years, my focus on this research had a singular purpose—to answer once and for all the numerous questions that had plagued me for decades. "Who was really to blame for the black hole in my young life? Was it me, or was it him? Or was it larger forces that shaped the context of both of our lives?"

An Iowa newspaper reporter during the early 1950s described Anthony Sainz as the "Famed Medic of Cherokee."[46] His fame for psychotropic drug development began at the end of 1954, just months before he left Iowa. A news wire story about the 121st meeting of the American Association for the Advancement of Science in Berkeley, California, reports about his research on human subjects with a drug called chlorpromazine (the generic name for the patented brand drug, Thorazine). The Sainz study claimed that chlorpromazine "improved the condition of 70 percent of the persons treated.... Nearly 500 persons were treated in studies made by the Mental Health Institute of Cherokee, Iowa and the famed Langley Porter Clinic in San Francisco." Sainz was paraphrased as saying that "chlorpromazine is not only safe but tends to counteract the mental confusion normally produced by a sedative."[47] (More recent and rigorous research has shown that such antipsychotic medications can increase the risk of death, particularly in elderly patients, from cardiovascular complications or infectious illness such as pneumonia.)[48]

Within two years, Sainz had gone from extolling the virtues of lobotomies to becoming, "one of three pioneers in the country in developing the new drugs for use in mental illness," according to an article about Sainz's speech at Iowa State Teachers College on "Growing Up Mentally Healthy and Strong."[49] Another 1955 newspaper column refers to Sainz's research with reserpine.[50] In September of that year, Sainz's new reputation as a pioneer in drug research took him to New York State, where he joined the staff at Marcy State Hospital near Utica. There, he continued his experiments, researched articles and arranged public appearances.

Eager to demonstrate what were considered as advancements in the care of the mentally ill, Marcy State Hospital heavily promoted the arrival of Dr. Sainz. During the late 1950s and 1960s, there were frequent articles in the daily newspaper *Utica Observer Dispatch* focusing on promising pharmaceutical discoveries being tested at Marcy, with extensive coverage of speaking engagements made by Dr. Sainz.

Through these newspaper accounts, we learn that after moving from Iowa to Oneida County in central upstate New York, Dr. Sainz and his wife Julia set up house near Marcy and began putting down roots in the community of Whitesboro, New York. They joined the First Presbyterian Church where they eventually became lay leaders. Within time, Julia also became involved in the League of Women Voters and the local Republican Party.

By 1958, the *Syracuse Herald Journal* referred to Sainz as "one of the pioneer developers of the new drugs for mental illness in this country."[51] Between 1954 and 1970, there are numerous newspapers and journals reporting about Sainz's experiments on mental patients with chlorpromazine, reserpine, Methonalide, Thorazine, Librium, Proketazine, Nardil, and other psychotropic drugs. A 1957 article in the *Rome Daily Sentinel* describes Sainz speaking on the "Psychic Action of Antihistamines."[52] Another from 1957 shows a photo of Sainz accepting an award for "distinguished efforts in psychiatric research" from the Eastern Psychiatric Research Association.[53] In 1959, Sainz is quoted about the hazards of overdosing.[54]

A 1962 article in the *Utica Observer* quotes Marcy's Director, Dr. Newton Bigelow, about research at Marcy involving chronic and acute schizophrenia. "The team is delving into biochemistry, particularly of the brain, psychology, internal medicine, and clinical psychiatry," the article reports. Dr. Bigelow further stated, "Diagnostic techniques have been improving so that more and more ailments are being recognized as mental disorders." Bigelow also proudly stated that Marcy uses tranquilizers "by the carload," claiming they were leading to a decline in the numbers of hospitalized mental patients.[55]

In early 1963, Marcy State Hospital expanded its research division to include "biochemical programs and investigation into the use of psychophysiological electronic instruments." It was at this time that Anthony Sainz was appointed to head the new center.[56]

In addition to their interests in psychiatric medicine and pharmaceuticals, Anthony Sainz and his wife Julia were involved in local civic affairs, partisan politics and international affairs. Dr. Sainz was elected "permanent chairman" of the Whitesboro Committee for Education in 1961[57] and President of the Oriskany Rotary Club in 1962. He spoke before the Mohawk Valley branch of the American Association of University Women. His wife's letter to the editor published in a local newspaper indicates she was a registered Republican. In 1962, the local newspaper extensively covered remarks by Dr. Sainz—an expatriate Cuban—about President John F. Kennedy's momentous decisions regarding the Cuban missile crisis.

Amid all of this media coverage, Dr. Sainz was always presented as a highly qualified and unquestioned authority, whether the topic was the cause of mental illness, the value of psychiatric drugs, development of a new type of antibiotic or U.S. foreign policy.

Throughout all of the developments in the career of Anthony Sainz, there was no public inquiry about the ethics of drug experiments on wards of the state residing in mental hospitals. Additionally, there was no public questioning of whether the burgeoning pharmaceutical industry was having an undue influence on claims about psychotropic drug effectiveness that were stated in news accounts or published studies.

And in an era without the instant communication of the Internet or database searches, it's doubtful that anyone in New York State knew how or why Dr. Sainz's reputation among some medical professionals at Iowa's Cherokee Institute had taken a turn one year before he moved to New York's Marcy State Hospital. It was not until medical records were revealed during a lawsuit in 1972 that New York authorities learned of a controversy in September 1954 among the medical staff of the Cherokee Institute. The disagreement arose over methods followed and medications ordered by Dr. Sainz for Ernest Triplett, a patient who had been admitted to the hospital for syphilis treatment, but who had become a police suspect in a child's murder.

While the murder investigation was underway and the controversy ensued in late September 1954, Sainz resigned from his post at Cherokee and took a job in Iowa City at the Veteran's Hospital there. It was just about one year later that he moved to New York State.

Unfortunately, the lawsuit that uncovered the controversy in Iowa did not come to conclusion until 1972, two years after I had become a patient of Dr. Anthony Sainz.

SAINZ'S SESSIONS

I HAVE FORGOTTEN MOST OF WHAT was discussed in my weekly sessions with Dr. Sainz, possibly due to the Trilafon or to the trauma of being considered insane by my family. I believe my parents were paying about $100 per session, which was an enormous fee in 1970 in Rome, New York. There are however, some memories of my time with the doctor that are impossible for me to erase.

Dr. Sainz did much of the talking himself, telling me that there were bad drugs on the street. Within a few sessions, he had frightened me into taking the medicine faithfully for my own good. While telling my mother that I was schizophrenic, he told me what my parents had told me initially—that the street drugs I had taken were tainted with chemicals that needed to be counteracted. In essence, he claimed that the Trilafon was an antidote for some type of poison in the marijuana I had smoked repeatedly or in the ineffective psilocybin I had taken one time with Paul.

His office was in a nondescript brick building across from what was then a Sears retail store in a strip mall shopping center on Black River Boulevard. Outside the office sat a nurse who I believe was his wife; she was a pleasant, attractive, well-dressed middle-aged American woman with well-coiffed hair. I could never understand how she could have married this gawky man who seemed like a cartoon character to me.

There were two rooms in the inner office. One was a typical psychiatric session room, with comfortable chairs opposite each other, a couch, and a box of tissues prominently displayed on the desk within an arm's reach of the patient's chair. There was another small room off the session room set up like a physician's examining room.

During one of my first visits to his office, he ushered me into the second, innermost room and told me to remove my shirt and bra and to put on a cloth gown as he left the room. As a 17-year-old unfamiliar with the conventions of psychiatric care, I didn't question his request. But when he came back into the room and gently pulled back the gown to touch my breasts and squeeze the nipples, my mind was filled with confusion and shame. I felt the way my dog looks when the vet does a rectal exam. I had the sense that something wrong was happening in this room, where no one other than me and this doctor were present. And yet, like my dog, I yielded to his authority and power, knowing deep down, once again, that resistance carried risks of much worse consequences. I avoided looking at him or down at my chest, completely uncomfortable with facing the reality of my situation. I had the vivid feeling that I was a lab specimen, like a rat held by the tail being prodded and probed for observation of my physical response.

My experience may seem like a clear case of malpractice or abuse of power in present time, but it seems that this was considered standard psychiatric protocol in many places in 1970. Unfortunately, the roots of this type of "treatment" run very deep, as the investigative book *The Shame of the States* by Albert Deutsch had documented about mental hospitals in 1948.

A few months after my post-hospitalization sessions with Dr. Sainz began in 1970, he told me that the CIA (Central Intelligence Agency) and the military were experimenting with LSD by giving it to soldiers and others. At the time, I thought that he was either out of touch himself, or being ridiculous in order to test my sense of sanity and reality.

But before the end of the 1970s, a Congressional committee and a Presidential Commission began an investigation that demonstrated that the tales Sainz told me were, in fact, true. Freedom of Information efforts yielded historical documents from the 1950s, '60s, and '70s, showing that the CIA had experimented with LSD and other drugs on its own staff, soldiers and mental patients, who were not told they were test subjects.[58] Files about these secret experiments that were not purposely destroyed in 1973 by the CIA are now in a national security archive at George Washington University titled "CIA Behavior Control Experiments Collection (John Marks Donation)," also known as MKULTRA files.[59]

In hindsight, it is bizarre that Dr. Sainz would tell his teen-aged patient—one whom he had diagnosed as psychotic—about CIA and military research into the effects of psychoactive drugs. Moreover, it raises the question of how Dr. Anthony A. Sainz knew about these experiments in 1970, unless he had been involved in them, since they were not publicly disclosed until Congressional investigations about them were initiated in 1975. In my efforts to research Sainz, I contacted the MKULTRA archivist, who said the names of individual doctors were redacted from the files that they had obtained, but the names of institutions were disclosed. She could not find Marcy State Hospital among the institutions named, but she did find a file labeled "Iowa State Hospital."[60]

At the time that I was a patient of Dr. Sainz, neither I nor the news media nor most American citizens knew anything about this CIA drug research. But it was a story that the doctor told more than once during my weekly sessions.

In another particular session with Dr. Sainz, I began to cry and talk about my sins. I'm not sure exactly what I said or how I said it, but I can vividly recall the alarmed and somewhat guilty look on his face. "You are not a bad person," he said. But by then, I had grown convinced that I must be evil—because I had been punished.

People who have never deeply embraced a faith like Roman Catholicism often have a difficult time understanding what it is like when you lose that faith. I had been a very good Catholic girl who went astray. While I was no longer a devotee, I could not escape the belief that God was issuing his judgment on me in this life instead of waiting until I died and went to hell. I had been found to be a heretic or even a witch, and I had been sentenced to a life with no capacity to feel joy, confidence, or hope.

Central to this emptiness was the knowledge that everyone else now thought I was crazy. My teachers, my family, my friends—even Paul the few times I saw him—all treated me like an emotional leper. No one knew that I was joking if I struggled to joke; everyone carried a tone in their voice as if I were three years old, or stricken with a terminal disease. I was locked inside their surmises about mental illness, even though I was not truly mentally ill. Given the dosage of medication I was taking, I'm sure I must have seemed strange and different than I was before. But years later, after discussing my experiences with numerous psychiatrists and psychologists, I came to realize that this strangeness was a result of the drugs, not of schizophrenia.

At the time, if I told people what was happening, that a doctor had put me on these pills and sent me to the hospital before seeing me, or if I described what he did and said during the sessions, they simply acted as if I were expressing delusions.

At many of these sessions, Dr. Sainz would attempt to hypnotize me. The first time he did this, I tried to comply but found that I couldn't stop myself from chuckling, despite the fact that the medication rarely enabled me to laugh.

This response seemed to anger him, and so I tried to follow along, as if in a charade. But now, in retrospect, I wonder if he had in fact successfully put me under hypnosis. To be in these sessions week after week, and have so little recollection of them seems strange, although it could be the result of the medication, my age, or a desire to suppress memories that were simply unpleasant.

Whatever took place in that doctor's office in Rome, New York, I lived in that nightmare on and off over a period of two years. The first time, I was under the age of 18, and I had no choice but to follow my parents' wishes or suffer worse consequences. The part that remains most difficult for me to understand is why I returned to Dr. Sainz of my own volition after my first year away at college.

GRADUATION

A good man in his darkest aberration,
Of the right path is conscious still.

– The Lord in *Faust*
Johann Wolfgang von Goethe

I HAD ALWAYS DONE EXCEPTIONALLY WELL on standardized tests. I took the National Merit test about six weeks after starting to take Trilafon, and about a week after being released from St. Elizabeth's psychiatric ward. So it's not surprising that my performance was not up to my usual standards, garnering not even an honorable mention.

When I took the test, I was extremely worried about what my scores would be. I knew that my future could hang on my answers, and I had trouble reading the questions, let alone responding to them. At the same time, I had other things to worry about. Word travels fast in a small town like Rome, New York. Despite my parents' efforts to shield me by sending me to a hospital 30 miles away, by the time I got back to school, I assumed that everyone had heard that I'd been hospitalized for some type of psychiatric breakdown.

Even if they hadn't heard the gossip, I was sure they could tell when I got back that I was not the same person who had left for Christmas break. But wherever I went, what had happened to me was an elephant in the room—something that no one mentioned, something that made my RCH friends hesitant to hang out with me, something that made even my teachers act awkwardly in front of me.

Despite all the strangeness, I did my best to maintain my focus on my schoolwork and continue my extracurricular activities. I still cheered with the squad and sang with the chorus. In English class with Father Stephan, we were all being pushed to conclude our senior year with a college-level term paper. Allowed to choose our focus from a list of literature, I selected Goethe's *Faust*.

I thought I would identify with Faust, having tried earlier in the school year to learn about witchcraft, which I knew would brand me among Catholics as having a Satanic bent. But the fact is, I had a lot of trouble following Goethe's poetry, whether due to the medication, a poor translation, or my own intellectual and spiritual immaturity. It was far more difficult than I had imagined to alternatively digest, analyze and write creatively about Faust. I thought it would help me to better understand my curiosity about the dark side and the terrible repercussions that had resulted thus far. But it was no more revealing to me at the time than Shakespeare's *King Lear* would have been in old English.

From a teacher who had consistently graded me with A's throughout three years of English classes, I received a tepid B-minus for the final paper. In fact, my grades for my entire senior year were less stellar than the previous three years. Having been well in the lead for valedictorian over a young man whose IQ outstripped mine, I stumbled at the end of the race and finished second. As a result, I still had the opportunity as salutatorian to address my class, their parents and mine, and teachers at graduation in June 1970.

Father Karlen, the school disciplinarian, reviewed all student speeches in advance and my address was found to be acceptable. But like most writers, I was still editing the morning of the speech, inserting additional explanatory phrases in the copy I was taking with me to read. None of these additions contained any profanity or slander, but they did express my personal opinions more clearly than the original version, including views about the Catholic Church. When I arrived at the theater where the ceremony was taking place, I learned that I had to give my copy of the speech to one of the sisters so that it could be placed in a binder at the podium with all the others.

Five minutes after I gave the copy to Sister Rose, I stood in line in my white graduation robe and cap with my classmates. Father Karlen came storming up to me, grabbed me by the arm and yanked me out of the procession line. He had the copy of my speech waving in his hand, with my additional comments blackened out.

"What do mean by adding these comments at the last minute, Wagner?" he shouted.

"I was giving examples," I stuttered, "trying to liven it up, explain myself better."

"Well, you're a spiteful, manipulative person, and you should be ashamed of yourself. You'll read this version, as we agreed in advance."

I held back tears of rage, and my entire body shook as he pushed me back into line. My high-school salutatory address had been censored, and he had ascribed evil motives to my attempts to improve it and express myself honestly. The line began to move and soon the RCH class of 1970 took their seats at the front of the auditorium.

When it was time for me to step up to the podium, I resolved to do my best to recall the phrases that were blackened out. In the first few minutes, my graduation cap kept sliding off my head. Finally, I said, "Excuse me," and removed it with a smile, leading the audience to break into laughter. This moment of comic relief helped to relax me, but I could only remember the first of the added comments, so I read the redacted version before me. My father's friend, who ran the local radio station, broadcasted and recorded the graduation ceremony, and I still have my original handwritten speech that was approved. Later that day, he gave me a copy of the speech on tape, which I also still have.

Linda Wagner's Salutatory Speech, Rome Catholic High School, June 1970

> My comments today are directed to my fellow class-mates, my dearest friends.
>
> From growing with all of you for the past four years, I know we are a class that loves good times. I warn you now that the future holds a world which threatens that fun, a world of repression, of division, of hatred, and of war. Yet I truly feel that we can hang on to our good times. How? By remaining as adolescents who will keep their dreams alive.
>
> The world outside belongs to a generation from whose hands we will take the reins. We have been called ni-hilists and have been claimed to be ready to destroy a society which we cannot replace. Yet we know, as D.T. Suzuki says, that "negativism is sound as method, but the highest truth is an affirmation."

Our affirmation is freedom—freedom to be all that we are and hope to be. This kind of freedom does not flow from any external system but from within, from the heart. It is present, however stifled, in every society. Our generation in our country has a monopoly on this kind of freedom and we will put it to use.

As we meet the future, each of us will exercise this freedom in a unique way. In so doing we will become part of a movement that is sweeping our nation. We have long been sheltered from this movement but we now must encounter it face to face. It is the movement of a people that are vibrant with life and hope. It is a movement that believes that we can attain love, freedom, peace, and full life. It is a movement that achieves its goals through its very struggle to attain them. It is composed of people who look upon life with the fresh, hopeful outlook of children.

My hopes today are idealistic. They are the hopes of one who has not become embittered with the so-called reality of life. Not yet, that is. But do we ever need to accept this reality? Must we grow to a maturity in which our childlike hopes cannot be realized? Once we reach that maturity we will stop striving as millions before us have done.

Yes, I ask you to remain as children, for only then can you gain the kingdom of heaven. I ask you to remember as the years pass that life should be enjoyed. Don't blindly accept the so-called reality of life. Don't give up your dreams.

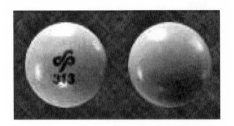

Trilafon – from www.drugs.com.

From Utica, NY *Observer Dispatch*, August 24, 1962

Reconstruction of Cuba
Should Be U.S. Aim: Sainz

By WALTER OSSENFORT

Dr. Anthony Sainz, research director at Marcy State Hospital, looked beyond the current Cuban tension last night by saying the United States "should now start planning the reconstruction of Cuba."

"This is where our great opportunity lies," the former Cuban governmental official said in an interview before an address before the Utica Discussion Group in the Strebel Student Center, Utica College.

The U. S., he said, has the "opportunity to make Cuba a showcase of democracy to the whole world."

He said: "We're going to have war, one way or another, with either Russia or Cuba. There will have to be a fight."

The United States, he said, "can start rebuilding Cuba by training the Cuban exiles in America to take over Cuba again."

Dr. Sainz, who has lived in America since 1947, said the "Cuban exiles should have special attention." They should be "given something to help make them a cohesive, functioning group."

* * *

COMMENTING on President Kennedy's action on Cuba, he said, "It is high time that the government has taken positive measures."

Dr. Sainz said the action would "strengthen the hand of the Latin American countries. Now they have a loud voice, instead of a craven voice, behind them.

"The Latin American countries," he said, "are afraid of being on the losing side. It is not a question of loyalty. They want to preserve their nations and try to lean to the stronger side."

He noted that the Russians "are making the Latins lean to them to make America look weak."

The 47-year-old phychiatrist said the naval quarantine of Cuba will help dispel the belief that the United States "was not determined to use full measures."

"The principle of moderation and arbitration is strictly of Anglo-Saxon origin," he said. This principle is "all right if it is understood" by the Latin American mind.

Dr. Sainz said that moderation also could "give the impression you're afraid." He said many Latins believed that "half-measures fail."

* * *

HE SAID he could not predict how the Cuban people would react to the quarantine. "Right now, Cubans will do what the Russians want them to do."

"They are being held in check by the bayonets" of the Castro government. And many feel, he believes, "that nobody wants them, anyway."

Dr. Sainz, who lived in Cuba during the 1930's and early 1940's to obtain his college education, said that "right now, Cuba must be written off."

"Cuba," he noted, "will be hurt no matter what happens. That is why America should begin to plan reconstruction of Cuba now."

The former director of medical services for a United Nations agency admitted that he was being "fatalistic" by assuming that war would result from the American quarantine of the Caribbean island. "This business has been planned by the Communists, that I know of, since 1933," he said.

"Cuba is the crossroads of the Americas," he said. "Geographically, it controls southeastern United States, the northern part of South America and Central America. Cultural and trade routes converge there."

He said Cuba was very strategic. It has been the ideal place for saboteurs to operate f r o m" because there have been no passport or quota restrictions between the United States and Cuba.

DR. SAINZ, born in Havana, was raised and educated in New York City. He returned to Cuba in 1931 to attain four different college degrees. He earned AB and BS degrees from the Provincial Institute, Havana, and went on to earn a Ph.D. in 1939 and his medical degree in 1941.

He held various Cuban government positions and practiced medicine in Cuba and Europe. He is an American citizen.

Dr. Sainz said he was critical of the United States for "not talking firm steps sooner. If this had been done before, it would not have required a blockade."

Commenting further on foreign policy, he said that "it's not just the dollars we can give them. Human nature thrives on hope."

Dr. Anthony Sainz
. . . "there will have to be a fight"

he Again

its will get an extra hour of is, if they remember to turn signaling the closing out of nother year.

plan in which clocks are set d Time during the summer nes one hour later.

ght Saving Time is from the ast Sunday in October.

s back that hour this coming e start of the winter season.

confused on whether to turn you have to do is this: When Saturday night — or early :o turn that alarm clock back :t the sack at 11 p. m. Satur-10 p. m., settle back and en- ber you lost last April.

d Daylight Saving Time in law in 1919. However, many

light Saving Time again was States. Since that time, the light during the summer has ndividual states or cities. we adopted the use of Day- r-around basis.

change will be television and some public transportation

to Hear Out Teachers,
Board Group Warned

Anthony A. Sainz suddenly becomes a local expert in foreign policy during the Cuban missile crisis in 1963.

VII

REPAIR, RENEW, RELAPSE

LEAVING HOME

ABOUT EIGHT WEEKS BEFORE MY HIGH school graduation, President Richard Nixon announced that U.S. troops would invade Cambodia. Only a few days later, members of the Ohio National Guard fired into a group of student demonstrators on the campus of Kent State University. Four unarmed students were killed, making it even clearer than before that a form of civil war had erupted once again on U.S. soil. The deaths during the previous decade of black and Jewish civil rights workers and assassinations of the Kennedys, Malcolm X and Martin Luther King were now joined by the killing of white middle class students by the U.S. military on heartland American soil.

At that time, my sister Carol was working as a counseling psychologist at a lab school for children ranging from toddlers through 12th grade on the Kent State University campus. An energetic and intelligent 28-year-old woman, Carol was in the midst of the campus upheaval as it erupted in May 1970. She recalls that the scene on campus had grown crazy after Nixon announced the Cambodian invasion and students had begun protesting on a Friday by smashing windows in local businesses. Suddenly, the National Guard was in full force on the campus and in the small town of Kent, Ohio, with helicopters overhead and armed soldiers visible everywhere.

The next Monday, there was a bomb threat at the lab school where Carol worked. The young son of a visiting professor from Czechoslovakia attended the high school, and the professor, sensing that the situation had grown terribly dangerous, had rushed to join his son inside the lab school just before the building was locked down. Carol remembers sitting there with the Czech professor as he said, "This is just like when the Russians invaded my home country." At about that time, the Guard opened fire on the college students outside.

While this was the immediate environment of Carol's life at that time, it was the breaking-news environment on televisions in living rooms across the U.S., including that of me and my parents. I identified with the students who had been protesting against the war in Vietnam and those who had been shot and killed by soldiers. My parents, having lived through World War II, identified with the boys in uniform, whom they saw as protecting our country from communist invaders who were trying to steal the minds of the nation's young people. Carol, surrounded by the chaos, was merely left shocked by the tragic results.

Nevertheless, the frightening political environment did not divert Carol from her summer travel plans, and lucky for me, she needed a companion for that year's trip. Having traveled across the U.S. and Europe with friends during previous vacations, she decided that it would make a fine graduation gift to include me in her plans to camp out across Canada. She thought I would benefit from time away from my parents and the judgmental comments they made about me whenever she talked with them on the phone. She also had some concerns, as a counseling psychologist, about the psychiatrist who'd been treating me with drugs.

With a tent, two sleeping bags, and a couple of bags packed with clothes, we set out in her Saab. From Oneida County in

New York State, we headed east, then north toward Montreal in early July. I was still taking the medication at that point, but the escape from my parents and Dr. Sainz proved to be a healthy development.

The highlights of the trip that I recall best include seeing a traveling theater troupe in near nudity perform *Hair* on the streets of Toronto, and watching a real rodeo during the Calgary Stampede in Alberta. We discovered a field covered with yellow and orange wildflowers by Lake Louise in the Canadian Rockies, and took the train north from Winnipeg in Manitoba all the way to Churchill on the Hudson Bay. It was there we saw native Canadians and the whales in the Bay that enabled them to make a living in a stark and barren land.

But most importantly, I remember Carol urging me to talk about my hopes—about things I'd learned in school, favorite artists, music and more. While we drove across the Canadian countryside, I heard Canadian singer Anne Murray singing "Snowbird" on the radio time and again. And in those spots where radio waves were weak, Carol would ask me to sing Joni Mitchell's "Big Yellow Taxi" urging me to belt out, "Don't it always seem to go that you don't know what you've got 'til it's gone?"

By the time we had finished this trip, which was the longest I had been away from home my entire life, I felt confident that I could go away to college in September with no problem. I also decided, without telling anyone, that after I arrived at school, I would forget about Dr. Sainz and stop taking the drugs he'd prescribed.

On Labor Day weekend, my father drove me and my trunk full of clothes, sheets, and towels south about an hour to Binghamton, where the State University of New York had purchased the formerly private Harpur College. Two other young women and I tried to cram our things into a dorm room in Endicott Hall that was designed for only two students. When it was time to say goodbye, my father's eyes teared up as he gave me one of his huge bear hugs. Despite the previous year of family turmoil and inner anger, I returned the hug and patted him on the back as I did when I was a little girl. I empathized with my Dad and felt the poignancy of this moment, but I also thought I was ready to move on with my life.

As his car drove away, I felt relieved and excited to be there. It was a place filled with people who spoke and dressed like me and blasted out Bob Dylan, Jimi Hendrix and Jefferson Airplane from their dorm-room windows.

FIRST YEAR OF COLLEGE

UNLIKE MANY OF MY CONTEMPORARIES, I began traveling to a new sub-culture before going away to college, while still housed within the larger, so called "straight culture" of my parents, high school and hometown. Now, at Harpur, the environment was dominated instead by the sub-culture. I felt that I was stepping into the future and shedding the past.

The first big change I made was that I completely stopped taking the medication that Dr. Sainz had prescribed. During my first semester, both my body and mind felt the joy of release from an invisible cage. Since no one at Harpur knew me before, they could not have seen the difference. But I experienced a very basic sense of liberation, more intense than most college freshman would have felt upon leaving home.

My dorm was one of the first to allow co-ed housing. The second floor was for guys, the third floor for girls. I had two roommates—Susan from Long Island and Kay from Brooklyn. Susan had a boyfriend who was one of the bigger drug dealers on campus—he kept many students supplied with weed and hallucinogens, such as small cylindrical-shaped pills of "Orange Sunshine" LSD. Kay was a feminist from Hunter High School in NYC, the grandchild of anarchist Russian Jews who had settled in NYC. Next door to us on our floor was a married couple,

Arden & Greg, Jewish intellectuals from NYC who had become involved with Renaissance revival. Down the hall was Teresa, a beautiful, gangly young woman from rural upstate NY. She and her roommate could not get along and I often played peacemaker with them.

Despite all the chaos that surrounded college campuses in that era, I was a very conscientious student. I woke up early every morning and studied before attending all of my classes, and pulled down good grades.

At that time, the drinking age was 18, so when I finished my schoolwork after dinner, I often headed over to the on-campus pub for a beer or two. My Plato & Aristotle Professor, Tony Preuss, sometimes held his class in the pub and bought us a pitcher of beer to drink while we waxed on about Platonic ideals and the Socratic method.

Most of the African-American students were from New York City. At the time, black students on our campus shared a version of Malcolm X's theory that segregation was far better for their empowerment than integration. As a result, the bottom floor of my dorm, called the Black Power Corridor, was strictly reserved for African-Americans.

Now that I was on my own, I developed a fairly outrageous style—I bought a bright orange winter coat with fake fur and burnt orange work boots for the winter. One male friend used to call me "John" since my glasses and shiny brown hair reminded him of singer-songwriter John Sebastian. My friend June nicknamed me "Orange" because of the coat.

I also developed a habit of indiscriminate promiscuity. While this was not uncommon for young women during an era of accessible birth control and sexual revolution, I operated in a nearly robotic fashion when it came to sex. The encounters were neither physically satisfying nor emotionally fulfilling. Often they occurred while I was drunk or stoned. Sometimes, I would cry hysterically afterwards. Other times, I would pass out and not remember what had happened. Observers might have wondered what led that young girl to have so little respect for herself? Had she been assaulted or abused as a child?

If challenged, as I was by a former high-school classmate, I would argue that I was the new norm—expressing freedom from any constraints. Internally, it felt as if I'd been thrown into a pool of water and I was just swimming as fast and furiously as I could.

One night during my first semester, I decided to drop a "barrel" (one cylindrical shaped pill) of "Orange Sunshine" LSD by myself. There was a well-reviewed theater production on campus that night performed by a traveling troupe of actors. About an hour before the show, I "dropped" the acid alone, violating a cardinal drug use rule that you should never trip alone on acid. I was still thinking and behaving relatively normally when I got to the show, with only a few dollars in my pocket and no ID on me. The show was a fabulous amalgam of childhood fairy tales, Native American music, and political and social commentary that criticized the U.S. for betraying the Indian nations and for fighting the Vietnamese. By the show's intermission, I was, as we said at the time, "tripping my brains out" but in a happily excited way, not in a fearful way. By the end of the show, I was still happy, but I did not know where I belonged or what day it was. I remained in my seat after everyone in the audience had left and the only people remaining were the actors.

Several of the actors came up to me to ask me if I was all right. I told them I had taken LSD, and that I had "lost my identity." They asked my name, and I was unable to answer. Since they often saw audience members in my condition, they decided they could not leave me there alone. They took me with them in their van to the house where they were staying, and put me to bed in one of the rooms there. I fell into a deep sleep filled with strange dreams, and in the morning, I awoke to bright sunshine on bedroom walls that were painted orange. I believed at the time that this was divine intervention—since my nickname was Orange, and the walls were orange, I thought that the actors were some type of angels. They fed me a healthy breakfast and asked again if I could remember my name. By then, I knew I was "Orange" and remembered my given name and where I lived on campus. They drove me back to my dorm, and wished me well.

This type of event was not unusual in the chaos that was campus life at Harpur in those years. I'm sure there were many students who did not do drugs or drink, but after my experiences with Dr. Sainz during my senior year in high school, I seemed drawn to self-destructive behavior once I was on my own. One night, I drank an entire bottle of wine by myself, another night I split a fifth of vodka with a girlfriend, and I sometimes had sex with total strangers while intoxicated. I went to parties off campus where I would find myself among many guys but very few girls, narrowly escaping gang rape by young college men—both white and black—more than once.

And yet, even with all the anarchy in my social life, I was developing constructive and healthy skills, habits and knowledge at the same time. Because my school had a physical education requirement, I learned to swim properly for the first time in my life during that first semester at college. During the second term, I learned the basics of fencing from Paul Pesthy, a Frenchman who was a former national fencing champion. I worked out vigorously in his class and helped to challenge his firm belief that women did not belong there. From on-campus resources, I learned about the dangers of eating too much sugar and overly refined foods, and the benefits of whole grains and raw fruit and vegetables. I joined a women's consciousness-raising group, where I gained a new perspective on women's lives and learned about aspects of women's history that were not part of school texts.

Overall, I remember my first year in college as an exhilarating and expressive time. I fell in love with philosophy and logic, moving from the indoctrination of twelve years of Catholic religious classes to open vistas of ethical, existentialist and solipsistic studies. Led by professors who encouraged critical thinking rather than unquestioning acceptance, I came to understand Catholicism as just one set of the world's religious concepts that had been shaped by the political history of the Jewish people, Greek culture and the early Roman and "Holy Roman" Empires.

I struggled with calculus, puzzled over anthropology and tried but failed at theater, which had been one of my strengths during high school. I found a graduate student to give me piano lessons. I wrote poetry, rode my bike and took the bus to the apartments of acquaintances who lived off campus. I did my best to figure out who I was and what I wanted to do, where I wanted to go with my life.

But near the end of the spring term, I began to feel oddly out of sorts and uneasy. This sensation was emotional and mental, but it was also intensely physical, as if my nerves were crawling with bugs. At the time, I did not even speculate that I might be experiencing some withdrawal from the Trilafon that I had stopped taking a few months before. Instead, I began to hear, figuratively, the voice of Dr. Sainz telling me that I would have breakdowns throughout my life if I didn't take the medication he had prescribed. And something deep inside me, perhaps planted during his sessions of hypnosis, gave me the urge to numb my mind.

Relapse Summer

When I first got home for the summer break after my first year away at college, my sense of unease began to ratchet upwards. I kept it at bay during the day, focusing on my work in the bakery at my father's store. The job was boring in many ways, but working with people kept it interesting. One of the women who worked with me was Jenny, an attractive divorcee who some say distracted my father, especially after hours at the bar nearby. She was always very kind as she trained me, and at the time, I did not suspect that she might be turning my father's head or worse. Customers came up and asked for bread, donuts, cinnamon rolls, large half-moon or chocolate chip cookies, colored Italian sugar cookies by the pound, and other special pastries that you could only get at the Mohegan store. At first, I sampled my favorites among the goodies, but I soon grew tired of the smell of sugar and butter.

After work, I would hang around with friends who were home from school. We'd often go bar-hopping at night, or just gather at someone's house to listen to music and talk. By that time, even my innocent girl friends from Rome Catholic High had lost their virginity and started smoking pot. But it was better for them that they had waited to experiment until they had left home, unlike what I had done.

I usually enjoyed my friends and myself during these out-
ings, but after I went home and turned on the television to watch
late-night TV, my mind would start to race. One night, I was
watching the Dick Cavett show. He was interviewing someone
from a newly founded environmental group, who was explaining
that our environment was plagued with poisons—in our air, our
water, and soil, and because it was in the soil, it was in our food.
Toxic chemicals had permeated the protective skin of the earth,
and there was no way to escape them; these chemicals were killing us and we had to stop them.

Rather than hearing this interview as it was intended—as a
call to activism—I heard it as a prediction of imminent doom of
the entire world. Given the intensity of the speaker and the images he painted, this is, in retrospect, understandable. Awareness
of environmental hazards was just beginning to spread and we
had little understanding of how they might be affecting us.

The problem was that my reaction, rather than intellectual,
was instinctual. As in any situation when a threat has an animal
backed into a corner, my body reacted physically with classic
fight-or-flight responses. My heart rate sped up, my breathing
quickened and I broke out in a sweat, hyperventilating and feeling
faint. It was many years before I learned that these internal sensations and external symptoms were associated with a panic attack.
All I knew then was how disturbed and out of control I felt.

As the days passed, this scene repeated itself over and over,
night after night. I realized that I needed help from someone,
some place to get it under control.

Unfortunately, at this point, less than a year after ending my
contact with Dr. Sainz, I was plagued by the fears that he had
instilled. When I reached out for some way to soothe myself, I
found myself overwhelmed by profound self-doubts. Planted the

previous year, they had taken root in the intervening period, and were now running rampant through my mind—like an invasive species in a garden.

Dr. Sainz had told me over and over that I was mentally ill, that I would be mentally ill for my entire life, and that I would suffer from repeated psychotic breakdowns after intermittent remissions. Since I will never know whether he had in fact hypnotized me successfully, I'll never know whether these thoughts were even more deeply engraved in the boulder that he had tied around my mind.

This, above all else, was the most corrupting influence from my encounters with Dr. Sainz. While I fought on an intellectual level against accepting his faulty diagnosis, I had been conditioned to doubt my own sanity on a more fundamental emotional level.

And so, when I began experiencing these repeated anxiety attacks late at night—making it difficult for me to sleep—I wanted nothing more than to quiet my racing mind. It may be that these episodes were themselves a neurological response, a type of delayed withdrawal symptom from ending the use of the Trilafon nine months earlier. But it's also likely that they were a psychological response to the traumatic experiences I had encountered during treatment by Dr. Sainz the previous year. It's even possible that these nervous outbreaks were simply the emergence of a newly anxious personality, with a level of anxiety that could easily be treated today with a few months of cognitive behavioral therapy.

Whatever their origin, the anxiety attacks led me back to Dr. Sainz and Trilafon. I knew that Trilafon would deaden my mind, and that's what I wanted. I wanted to turn off my stormy feelings, my mental gyrations and my horrifying imagination.

After being home for a couple of weeks, with this anxiety eroding my sleep and creeping further and further out of the late night and into the day, I told my mother I wanted to go back to Dr. Sainz. Of course, she said yes.

Dr. Sainz did not seem at all surprised to see me. When I told him how I had been feeling, he quickly reached for his prescription pad but he no longer seemed interested in talking with me. It was as if I had served some useful purpose the previous year, but that purpose was no longer in effect. He encouraged me to get the prescription filled and to let him know if there were any problems, but I don't recall that he scheduled any further appointments.

When I said that I thought I should leave home and go back to live in Binghamton with friends for the rest of the summer, he said that was fine. I had one other business item to discuss with him. I had never obtained my driver's license when I lived at home. I was about to take a driving test, but the Department of Motor Vehicles required a special form if you were under the care of a psychiatrist. Rather than ignoring this as many people might, my Catholic upbringing dictated that I follow the procedure required by law. I gave Dr. Sainz the form and without hesitation, he signed it and handed it back to me.

There before me for the first time, on a four-by-five-inch state agency form, was Dr. Sainz's diagnosis of my alleged condition. "Undifferentiated schizophrenia." I stepped back, dropped my arm with the paper in my hand and looked at him. He had already turned away to an incoming phone call and I walked out the door, trembling.

I learned much later in life that Dr. Sainz was a pharmacological researcher, and that there is a good chance that I was one of his subjects during my senior year in high school. Given his list of publications, I may have been part of the data he was gathering for an article that would have been published by the time I returned to him a year later. With that publication behind him, there would be no reason to meet with me, despite the fact that he was putting me back onto a powerful anti-psychotic medication. Although the dosage was now lower than it had been a year-and-a-half before, it was still extremely high by today's standards, even for a real schizophrenic. The effect of the drug on a relatively normal brain was immense, akin to the effects of Parkinson's disease.

I got the prescription filled and began taking it. At the same time, I told my parents I had made arrangements with fellow students to share a house in Binghamton and to work during the rest of the summer for a Psychology professor who was conducting research on campus. They seemed happy to hear that I felt up to moving back to Binghamton.

Within a week, I was back in my college home. Initially, my living situation was fun, since we were college kids sharing a big house and often invited our friends over. I liked my roommates Teresa and Abbie, and tolerated the fact that they rarely helped me clean the house. My job with the professor was tedious but simple, involving the recording of data manually in the years before computers were in use for such tasks. The professor was testing white mice for their responses in a behavior modification experiment.

The bigger challenge became that within a few weeks, the Trilafon began to have powerful side effects. My jaw and mouth would move uncontrollably at times, which made me look bizarre. I had also developed a stutter for the first time in my life. When I called Dr. Sainz to ask about this, his wife/assistant told me I should go to a doctor in Binghamton and that they would talk with that doctor about what to do.

The on-campus doctor advised me to decrease the dosage, which I did. He also prescribed something else in an effort to counteract the side effect. For the rest of the summer, I took these medications on and off, believing intermittently that they were harming me on the one hand, but fearing on the other hand that I would go crazy if I didn't take them. While I lived as normally as I could, the stutter did not disappear and occasionally the dyskinesia, or uncontrolled movements, would surface again. Some of our acquaintances made fun of me, although Teresa and Abbe would always rise to my defense.

When the job ended that summer, I decided to go back home for a while before school started, hoping that I could address the medication problem. Dr. Sainz urged me to continue on with it, despite the side effects. As someone not yet 19, I did not know where else to turn. Within a couple of weeks, it was time to go back to college for the fall term. This time, I did so not with excitement but with trepidation.

I arrived at Roosevelt Hall, my new dorm where I should have been happy since it was more modern and I had a single bedroom within a suite. I had arranged the previous spring to share the suite with June, the lovely young woman who had originated my college nickname "Orange." She was always open and kind, and she had a Japanese-American boyfriend who was compassionate and bright and shared my interest in Heidegger's philosophy, although he had a more critical approach to it than I did.

Despite all of these positives, I was confronted every day by the uncertainty about taking the prescribed medication and embarrassed by the side effects it had. But more disturbing, I had become enmeshed in a web of darkness, rarely laughing or smiling, and never feeling any sense of joy about things that had once thrilled me. I now realized fully that a psychiatrist had diagnosed me as a schizophrenic, and had declared this diagnosis on a state document. At this point, my mind was not just numbed by the

Trilafon, but I was, in fact, suffering from a deep clinical depression. I felt a complete collapse of self-confidence, aware that my family believed I was doomed to a life of mental illness, and convinced by Dr. Sainz and my parents that they must be right.

I was suddenly four years old again, inside a locked trunk, with a dark specter of evil rising up from the shadows, ready to strike me down.

DARKNESS FALLS 1971

IT WAS A TYPICAL CLOUDY DAY in Binghamton. An autumn Sunday on campus, late-afternoon quiet surrounded me in the dorm as my suitemates were out and about on campus. The temperature outdoors was a comfortable 75 degrees, with a slight breeze blowing up the leaves on the ground.

In those days, we still used double-edged and single-edged razors to shave our legs and under our arms, before the special, safer razors of the late 20th century made their debut. After brushing my teeth, I took the case of single-edged razors out of the bathroom to my bedroom and set it on the bed. I changed into my faded blue jeans and a long-sleeved t-shirt, occasionally looking at the razors sitting on the comforter.

I went back into the bathroom to take another look at myself in the mirror. I was flat-chested, had acne and a big nose. As my mother had always said, my face wasn't pretty enough to wear my hair long and straight as I did, and I could be mistaken for an adolescent boy.

Moreover, I was unable to focus on my school work. I couldn't sleep well, worrying about whether or not Dr. Sainz had been right in diagnosing me as a schizophrenic. Ever the A student before, I had scored Cs and Ds in assignments the previous week. And I didn't really care. I didn't care about anything. I especially didn't care about myself.

So I put the case of razor blades into my pocket and packed a backpack with a pillow and a blanket, and strapped it on my shoulders. Even if anyone had been watching me, they would have seen nothing unusual. They would have seen a student, leaving her dorm with a backpack, maybe going for a walk or to the pub to meet a fellow student.

I walked for about a half-mile around the campus looking for the right spot, a place remote enough that no one would see me as dusk turned to dark. I finally found a good location just as the sun sunk below the horizon. It was in a ravine, well off the side of a road that was not used on the weekends, and I walked down to the lowest spot to make sure I couldn't see the road from there. I figured that even if a car came by, the driver would not be able to see me in the car's headlights. I took off my backpack and laid out the blanket, settling as comfortably as I could with my head resting on the pillow.

For a long while, I stared up at the sky, watching as orange, pink and purplish tints faded from the clouds on the horizon. I watched as the sky grew a darker and darker gray, until the breeze grew strong and pushed the clouds aside, opening a window to the blackness above.

No one knows where I am, I thought. *Whoever finds me will not be someone who knows me, which will be a blessing*. I did not want to hurt anyone. I just wanted to leave.

Taking the case of razors out of my pocket, I stared at it, thinking about how empty the sky looked, with only the first evening stars out. I felt that emptiness. I felt like the clouds that the breeze was pushing away. I felt like nothing.

I took a single blade out of the case with my right hand and pressed it horizontally across my left wrist, slicing the skin deeply enough to cut through the surface. Then I used my left hand to cut my right wrist. These were days before the Internet, when there were no easily accessible manuals on how to successfully cut your wrists. As a small amount of blood began to flow and the cuts produced some pain, I looked up again at the sky.

Nearly all the clouds had parted. The sky was now a deep dark blue and the stars had blossomed. As I stared at the sky, I imagined my dead body being picked at my birds, gnawed by wild animals, crawling with worms. I imagined the police telling my parents, and I saw them weeping together. I imagined the story in the newspaper, another Harpur College student commits suicide.

Suddenly, I burst into tears. They were tears for my own demise—grief for the sorry state of my heart, mind, and body. Fear for my soul.

"I can't do this," I said out loud. "I can't do this." And I began to cry even harder for my own failure to find an easy way out.

I must have lain there for another hour, sobbing until there was no water or salt left in my tear ducts. By the time I dabbed at my wrist to stop the bleeding and packed up the pillow and blanket, the wind had come up from another direction, and clouds covered the sky once again. I put on my backpack and headed back to the dorm, avoiding anyone I saw. But when I arrived, my suite-mate June was in the lounge and she asked, "Where have you been? Your eyes are all red. Are you OK?"

"I'm just feeling sick. Allergies or a cold or something," I said. "I'm going to bed." And I crept into my room, collapsed on the bed and stared at the ceiling until I fell asleep.

A few days later, my old friend Marilyn paid me an impromptu visit from the community college she was attending. I was not expecting or prepared to see her, but she had a day off and just showed up. She met me at my dorm, took one look at me, noticed bandages on my wrists and said, "We've got to get you out of here. What's the matter with this place?" I didn't have to tell her what was going on. She took charge.

"I'm living in a big house in Auburn with a bunch of other people—some of us are working, some going to school, some are doing both. You can come and live with us. It's like a commune—we share food and everything. It's a big, beautiful old house."

"What about school? What will I do in Auburn?"

"Linda, what are you doing here? You can't stay—this is terrible for you. Come with me, you can get a job waitressing or something, and register at the community college."

I was not in a state of mind to argue, and I was certainly ready for any type of escape. Although I had no energy, Marilyn was so enthusiastic, I believed she must be right. I packed up my things and we loaded them into her car. Within two hours, we were at Marilyn's place in Auburn. From there I called my parents and told them I was dropping out of school.

I also threw away forever the Trilafon pills that Dr. Sainz had prescribed.

Linda's sister Carol, before their trip across Canada during the summer of 1970.

College housemates (from left) Abbie, Teresa, and Linda at an off-campus house in Binghamton, NY, Summer 1971.

HONORED — Dr. Anthony Sainz, director of research at Marcy State Hospital, has been awarded the annual Eastern Psychiatric Research Association award for distinguished efforts in psychiatric research it was announced today. Dr. Sainz is chairman of the association's public relations committee. President of the group is Dr. Paul Hoch, state mental hygiene commissioner.

From Utica, NY *Observer Dispatch*, October 1963

State of New York
Department of Motor Vehicles

PHYSICIAN'S CERTIFICATE

This is to certify that:

Print
Name **Linda Mary Wagner**

Date of Birth

Print
Address   Rome, New York

has been under my professional care for

☐ HEART AILMENT   ☑ MENTAL ILLNESS

☐ OTHER (Please Indicate your Diagnosis)

_Chronic undifferentiated schizophrenia-
Has been in remission since June, 1970.
Was hospitalized for initial treatment at
St. Elizabeth Hosp., Utica, 1/29/70 → 2/10/70.—_

He(or she) has been treated for:

☐ Epilepsy   ☐ Convulsive disorder

☐ Fainting or dizzy spells   ☐ A condition causing unconsciousness

Would the patient's medical condition interfere with his(or her) safe operation
of a vehicle upon the highways of this State. ☐ Yes   ☒ 'No

I am ☑ a qualified Psychiatrist.
am not ☐

Doctor - Please Sign, as well as, Print, Type or Stamp your name and address and
give your New York State Certificate Number. In the event you are not licensed to
practice in this State, please indicate the State in which you are licensed and your
Certificate or Registration Number in that State.

Physician's Name | Physician's Certificate Number and State

Anthony Sainz M.D. | 095560

Physician's Address

3 Parkside Ct. Utica, New York   13501

Physician's Signature | Date

The diagnosis of Dr. Sainz becomes clear to Linda during the summer
of 1971.

233

**to help maintain
the ambulatory
schizophrenic patient**

TARACTAN®
(chlorprothixene)

Pharmaceutical ads such as these fill the pages of some psychiatric journals during the 1950s and '60s.

VIII

TURN, TURN, TURN

THE COLOR OF HOPE

A time to gain, a time to lose
A time to rend, a time to sew
A time for love, a time for hate
A time for peace, I swear it's not too late-

– Adapted from the *Book of Ecclesiastes*
(with the exception of the last line),
music by Pete Seeger in 1959

THE HOUSE IN AUBURN WAS A lovely turn-of-the-20th-century home located on a main thoroughfare, with high ceilings and unusually large rooms for a house of its era. While Marilyn and her housemates viewed it as a commune, there was no conscious structure as in some rural communes of that time, where residents made a commitment to work the land or practice a particular faith in the hopes of building a new world.

Rather, this was an island of anarchy in an increasingly chaotic outside world. Drugs were plentiful, schedules were ignored and lines of sexual propriety were blurred. Marilyn, as the household "earth mother," did her best to keep some order, but it was too hard to swim against the currents.

After a few weeks of living there and making no progress with looking for or finding a job, and facing a renewed feeling of despondence, I told Marilyn I had to go home. Realizing she had taken on more than she could fix by bringing me to Auburn, she understood and didn't try to make me stay. I can't remember whether she drove me to Rome or if my parents came to pick me up. But at some point that autumn, I found myself back at my parents' home.

I was engulfed in utter emptiness, blacker than the day that I carried razor blades off to a remote spot on campus. While my parents were there physically, I had detached myself from them emotionally in the course of the previous two years. I had nothing to say to them, and I'm sure they were puzzled about what to say to me. The lowest point during that time was a 36-hour period when I lay on the dark-brown tweed couch in the finished basement with the TV on in front of me. I got up only to go to the bathroom, on my way back picking up fast-food snacks and soda laden with calories, fat, and salt to bring back to the couch to devour. I fell asleep there and woke up with the TV on in the morning, and stayed there again throughout the next day.

After a day-and-a-half, something I heard or saw on TV, or perhaps discovered within myself, triggered me into realizing that I had nowhere to go but up. That night, I went back to my bedroom to sleep instead of remaining on the couch like a bump on a log. In the morning, I lay in my bed looking around at the room where I had spent all of my teen years. I reached a decision that might seem trivial, but in retrospect, I can see was significant. I decided that I wanted to paint my room in bright colors, and over breakfast, I convinced my mother that this was something that had to be done as soon as possible.

"We need more color in our lives," I told her. "Beige and off-white cream colors are so dull, so boring. Our society needs to accept more diversity, like the colors that Native Americans or Mexicans use." She didn't argue with me. After watching me do absolutely nothing for weeks, I am sure my mother was thrilled to hear that I wanted to do anything, even if my room had been freshly painted the year before.

That day, she drove me to Sears, the best place in the area to find the widest selection of paints at that time. I wanted vibrant shades of yellow and orange, but the pallet of indoor paints available in Rome in 1971 included only pastels. I accepted the compromise and chose a more subdued version of my imagined décor. Getting the paint was a step in the right direction, but I quickly fell back into a slump.

Luckily for me, one of my old friends Chris was on a break from school that week. She came to visit me and, like Marilyn, saw that I needed to get out of my current environment. She suggested that we take a trip with a fellow classmate named Dave to visit some other high-school buddies at their campus.

My old friends were in new environments facing both the excitements and the fears of college life. I could see that I was not alone in my struggles, even if mine seemed more extreme. Their encouragement also pushed me to start considering how I could turn the page on my past and move forward.

When I came back from the trip, I pulled together the paint, brushes, rollers and tape, moved and covered the furniture in my room, turned on the radio and started to work. The combination of music and physical labor that showed immediate results created a loop of positive energy. After seeing new color on the walls and adding a second coat to strengthen the tone, I decided that I could create an even brighter feeling with a colorful bedspread. At one of the local shops, I found a brilliant spring-green comforter with bright yellow and orange flowers, and matching curtains. It brought everything together and most important, conveyed cheer.

What was more significant about this activity than the result was the decision that lay beneath it. With no prescription medication, street drugs, or treatment other than the presence of my parents and the kindness of friends, I had chosen to close the door on the pain and sorrow of the previous two years and actively seek happiness. A bright bedspread and colorful walls were the expression of this choice. It was the beginning of a lot of hard work.

OFF CAMPUS

ONCE I PULLED MYSELF UP OUT of my deep depression, I began talking more with my parents. I took an art class at the local art center, practiced and played piano and exercised and visited with friends when they were home for holidays and school breaks. I stayed in touch with June, who told me she planned to move off campus in January and asked if I'd be coming back to school. I grappled with this decision, afraid of returning to the same environment that had surrounded my severe slump.

Over the phone, June—an unlikely optimist—argued with me about my hesitation to return to school. "Orange, you carry your emotional environment with you wherever you go. You can't pin that on Binghamton. If you're determined to change it, and it sounds like you are, then you will not be doomed to a repeat performance. And I'll be here to remind you of that. Besides, who else am I going to live with off campus?"

I started looking again at my college record thus far and at the courses being offered in the spring. I gained reassurance from Harpur that my incompletes would be dropped entirely from my record, and I grew excited about the prospects of taking new courses and living off campus. By early December, I felt bored, increasingly strong and self-confident, and ready to move forward. I registered for the spring term and began preparing to leave again for Binghamton.

When my high-school friends were home for Christmas, I exchanged handmade gifts with many of them. I had gained weight but had a pasty look, and I must have still appeared melancholic to old friends and family. Despite it all, there was a kernel of hope and determination inside, a spark of fighting energy. I had redeveloped some capacity to think about someone other than myself and appreciated the company of friends. I had fun playing with my nieces and nephews and embracing my own childish sensibilities, while simultaneously understanding that I was no longer a child myself.

After the holidays, I met with June to check out an apartment she had found. In the basement of a small apartment building in Binghamton, it had some high windows that let in a bit of outdoor light. As far as apartments go, it was cramped but spacious compared to a dorm. And it would be ours, complete with a kitchen.

"I'm ready to sign on. What do you say, Orange?" June asked me.

"It's not beautiful, but it's big enough and it's in the budget," I answered. "Let's go for it." After calling my parents to tell them about it and making sure it was OK with them, we signed the lease.

June took the single bedroom that was to the left of the front door, and I set up a bed in the living room opposite the front door, with a curtain rigged around it to give me some privacy. We had fun furnishing the apartment and equipping the kitchen with castoff furniture and kitchen gear from our parents, along with some curtains and chairs we found from secondhand stores. June's excitement about making our own little home was contagious, and I soon forgot about any anxieties I had in returning to school.

As we set up our apartment, I told June about my misadventures in Auburn, my defeated return home to my parents and my struggles to turn myself around. She filled me in on the previous term in Binghamton and how her relationship with her boyfriend had survived the summer. We had a few days before school started, and she convinced me to take the bus with her to Brooklyn to meet her parents.

When we walked into their apartment across from Prospect Park, her father, a tailor, was at a sewing machine. I had never before seen or even imagined a man sewing clothing, just as my mother could not imagine me as a girl learning carpentry. There was something hopeful for me in seeing a different model of gender roles, adulthood and family life than those I had witnessed growing up in East Syracuse and Rome. I began to understand in a more personal sense that the world could offer me many possibilities.

June and I had a good visit and returned to Binghamton to start the next semester.

THE SEARCH FOR A DOCTOR

MORE IMPORTANT THAN THE SEARCH WITH June for an acceptable off-campus apartment, I had decided to seek out a new doctor to help me put back together the many pieces of my crushed emotional and psychic health. I expected this process to be a simple matter of repeated visits to the campus psychological services office, but it proved to be much harder both emotionally and physically than I thought.

Between classes, I took what turned out to be only a first step by going to that office. Since I had not identified myself as imminently suicidal, a case of drug overdose, or a victim of battery or rape, I had to wait several more weeks to see a counselor for a visit. When I finally got in to see the counselor with a Masters in Social Work who was handling my case, he listened carefully and attentively to my story for about half-an-hour and then explained that they were equipped to handle only emergencies, while my case called for long-term therapy. He said he could provide me with a list of three private practitioners in the area—two psychiatrists and one psychologist—who were willing to take on new patients from the student population. The MSW also explained that this would mean fees for their services, which would necessitate informing my parents and obtaining their permission since I had no money of my own.

The list included a female psychiatrist who was a native of France. Having a woman doctor was my first choice, and the fact that I had studied French for four years made her seem even more appealing. Her office was on the bus route between my apartment and campus, so it would also be easy to get there on a regular basis.

To hedge my bets and have points of comparison, I set up appointments with all three—I'll call them Dr. A, Dr. B and Dr. C—making the appointment with the French woman, Dr. A, first. I was eager to get started, desperate for relief from the intense confusion I felt about who I was and from the sadness I suffered over my recent history.

My appointment with Dr. A was early on a day when I had no classes. When I arrived at her office and knocked on the door, she said, "Come in," without getting up from behind her large mahogany desk. She did not look up at me until I sat down in front of the desk. She was an attractive and trim woman in her late 30s who did not smile and seemed edgy. "I'm [Doctor A] and I presume you are Linda?"

"Yes."

"And what brings you here?"

I proceeded to tell her my story, and after about 20 minutes, she fired off a series of rapid-fire questions: Are you going to your classes? Do you sleep at night? Do you have any friends? Do you speak to your parents?

When I said yes to all of these questions, she paused for a moment and then said, "I don't have time for people like you who are not really sick. I treat people who are so mentally crippled that they can't possibly work or go to school. You are fine. You should just get on with your life." She got up and showed me the door.

After I got out onto the street and started walking, tears welled up in my eyes and down my face. I stumbled along, my vision blurry. While this doctor had affirmed that I was not mentally ill, her dismissal of my pain did not remove any of the grief, sorrow, or anxiety that had built up over the previous two years. I had called out to her for help and she, virtually, slapped me across the face saying, "Get over it," just in different words.

I had two more appointments scheduled—one with a male psychologist two hours later and one with a male psychiatrist the next day. I stopped at a diner to collect myself and do some school work before going on to the next appointment. His office was just a 15-minute bus ride from the diner, and when I arrived, I saw a sign on the door inside the waiting room that said, "I'll be with you in a moment. Please be patient." Within ten minutes he opened the door and introduced himself. He was young and seemed kind and open. I sat down in a large stuffed chair and told him about my situation, including the experience I had earlier that day with the female psychiatrist. He sat quietly for a few minutes, looked up and then down, and then directly into my eyes.

"Given your history with medication, I would recommend that you see a psychiatrist who would be more familiar with the effects of what you've been prescribed in the past. As a psychologist, I don't have that background." He must have seen the distressed look on my face. "Linda, let me assure you that if you find yourself with no other options, I'd be willing to take you on as a patient and do what I can. I just think you'd be better served with a psychiatric approach first."

I got up to leave, and he handed me a card. "Call me if you need me."

That night my sleep was restless. It had taken such monumental effort to get myself to these two appointments, and now I seemed no further along than I had been before I started. I tried to find encouragement in Dr. A's words, "You are fine. Get on with your life." But I did not feel fine, and her statements made me feel even weaker, insinuating as they did that my suffering was trivial and my needs negligible.

Dr. B was kind and compassionate, but he was a reluctant back-pocket option. What if Dr. C sent me on my way tomorrow? I searched inside myself to find the resources to overcome my past and move forward. I knew I had made some progress already, but I was still confused about what had happened to me. I did not know what was true, what mistakes I had made, why I had been diagnosed as I had or what this whole experience had done to me. I was not sure who I was or where I was going, and I was consumed by feelings of guilt, shame and fear.

After waking up several times that night, I fell into a deep sleep. In my dreams, I found myself locked in a room with a man in a white coat, struggling to get out. I finally dragged myself along the floor and through the door. When I looked down, I was shocked to see that I was covered in blood, cuts, and bruises as if I'd been pulled behind a moving car. I could not remember what had happened in there, and I felt stunned and puzzled that it seemed I had been assaulted. Gradually, inside the dream, I began to sense that I was safe in my bed and I'd wake up, glad the dream was over. But when I opened my eyes, I saw the door still in front of me, and I was back in the room with the man in the white coat, crawling along the floor, trying to escape. The same scenario repeated itself over and over within the dream before I would finally wake up in a sweat. This nightmare recurred for several months.

DOC ON THE HILL

My third and final option was Dr. Joseph Joel Friedman, who worked out of his home on the crest of a hill overlooking the Susquehanna Valley. There was no bus route near his house, so the only way I could get to his home office since I had no car was by foot or bicycle. I was fortunate that the weather was clear, sunny and cool the day of my first visit there.

Partly due to my college's requirement for physical education, I was in decent shape. But a 45-minute bike ride that is all uphill was a challenge, especially given that the bike had only one gear. When I got to Dr. Friedman's house, I was obviously sweaty and winded. The house was a lovely, dark, wooden structure in the architectural style of Frank Lloyd Wright, surrounded by mature fir and birch trees. The doctor greeted me at the door. With a full gray beard and mustache and sparkling eyes, he had the gentle manner of a grandfather. As I introduced myself and he took note of my appearance and bike, it seemed that I had earned his immediate respect.

"That's quite a steep ride to make on a bicycle."

"It sure is. I guess I really wanted to get here today." I noticed a bronze sculpture on the end table in the waiting room, a woman's figure with arms and face raised to the sky, her face twisted in agony, her body draped in a flowing robe. "What a beautiful sculpture. Who's the artist?" I asked.

"I made it," he said. "It's a Vietnamese peasant woman. I imagined that she has just seen her children killed in the war."

I raised my eyebrows, amazed to hear this compassion and sensitivity from someone of his age. With that, the respect was mutual. We chatted a few minutes as we stood in the waiting-room area. He asked me what year I was in college, and where I was from. I explained that my parents knew I was searching for my own doctor and were willing to pay his fees. He showed me into the next room, saying, "Let's not worry about money. First things first, please have a seat."

The room had a high window that allowed sunlight in, but the trees outside shielded the room's privacy. Sitting there gave me the sense that I was in a natural environment with all the peace that nature signified to me.

"What is so troubling that you rode all the way here on a bike to see me?" he asked.

By now, I had rehearsed my story twice with other doctors so I was succinct. "I was diagnosed as a schizophrenic by another psychiatrist two years ago when I was still living at home. I was given medication and hospitalized in a psychiatric ward before the doctor ever saw me."

"And how did this doctor decide you needed treatment?"

"On the basis of a meeting with my parents after they read my diary."

Dr. Friedman was silent for a moment, and then breathed a deep sigh. "I hope you realize that you've been subject to mis-treatment."

I tried to speak, "I...I...I..." but I started to cry instead.

He stood up to place a box of tissues in front of me and put a hand on my shoulder.

"Let it out. Go ahead."

He sat across from me silently while I cried for a few more minutes.

Finally, I was able to stop. "Sorry, it hurts to talk about this," I said.

"No apologies are necessary here. I want you to know that I have treated hundreds of schizophrenics over the years. There is no way that you are a schizophrenic. Who was this doctor?"

I explained about Dr. Sainz, told him about the Trilafon and the dosage I'd been prescribed, and described the hypnosis.

"Hypnosis can be an effective tool in the right circumstances, but whether your circumstances were right seems doubtful."

He listened to me for nearly an hour, and then he said, "Linda, you clearly need help and I believe I can help you. But you have to agree to some terms that I will set. First, you can't use alcohol or other illegal drugs if you're going to see me. If you're abusing substances like that, it will interfere with our progress here. Second, what I would also ask is that you help me understand what is going on with so many young people like you—why are you rejecting everything about our society? Can you agree to those terms?"

"Yes, I'll do my best," I said, though I was doubtful I could avoid having a couple of beers or smoking a little pot once in a while.

"Then we have a deal," he said, and reached out to shake my hand.

HILL SESSIONS

WEEK AFTER WEEK, I SLOGGED UP the long hill on my bicycle to see Dr. Friedman. In wet weather, I wore a rain poncho and in the heat of the sun in late spring and summer, I stopped frequently to drink water from a canteen and rest. I found shortcuts and on occasion, I bummed a ride up the hill with a friend, and walked down to the nearest bus stop after my appointment.

This was a case where getting there was at least a part of the fun. The bike rides and walks were not only a physical workout, but also they were a literal climb out of a pit of self-doubt and depression. When I got to Dr. Friedman's office, his skills and insights were like a welcome drink of cold water for my scorched emotions.

There were times that he simply listened quietly to my tales about Dr. Sainz for most of the session. But at the end, he would always reassure me that this other doctor had made grave errors in his practice, while pointing out that I had sometimes behaved self-destructively. He made it clear that my parents had been right in seeking out some type of help, but that they had been pointed in a direction that was, at best, mistaken and unfortunate.

I shared my dreams and nightmares with Dr. Friedman, who always seemed to interpret them silently before offering me a lesson with a different perspective on human behavior than those from which I had been raised and schooled. One night I woke up disturbed and frightened with beautiful string music ringing in my head. In the dream, I had been a cello that was playing itself. When I described to Dr. Friedman how upset this dream had made me, he probed, "Describe the feeling that you had when you awoke more fully. What was the reason beneath this fear?"

"I was doing something awful, but I loved the music and I felt torn."

"So you felt guilt when you woke up?"

I put myself back in the dream and the moment of waking up. "Yeah. Guilt. That's what it was. I felt guilty."

He was quiet for a minute. "You know, in some religions, masturbation and other sexual activity is seen as dirty and sinful. But in many other faiths and cultures, that same sexual activity is viewed as normal, healthy human behavior. You've come from a faith that sends very strong negative signals about sex. But you should understand that it is not wrong to have sexual feelings, and it is only human to act on those feelings. What is important is that you act with respect and caring for yourself and others. That you not force yourself on anyone, that you not harm yourself or allow others to harm you."

He told me about his love for his wife and their shared pleasure in intimacy. He asked if I gained real pleasure and satisfaction from my sexual encounters. I had to admit that my sexual experiences only seemed to fuel and frustrate my desire, rather than quench it.

"In sex, just as in the rest of life, you need to learn how to satisfy yourself. Once you know that, you can show a partner how to satisfy you. This is true not only physically but emotionally and intellectually."

There were some things about Dr. Sainz that I did not discuss with Dr. Friedman because I became aware of them myself only with the passage of time. And I was too embarrassed to describe to Dr. Friedman the time that Dr. Sainz had me undress and felt my breasts.

But after seeing him for several months, Dr. Friedman told me he had finally obtained some past medical records. He reaffirmed for me that the records indicated that I had not been properly screened, diagnosed, or treated. He apologized for the mistakes made by some in his profession.

He also told me that Dr. Sainz and a gynecologist I had seen in Utica had ordered a Barr chromosome test on me. This genetic test was developed by Dr. Murray Barr and was used first by the international Olympic committee in 1968 to determine the gender of athletes when it was in doubt. A Barr body is an inactive X chromosome in human cells that indicates normal female gender.[61] Dr. Friedman informed me that my test results were normal.

I was baffled. My breasts were small but they were clearly female. My genitals were clearly female, which the gynecologist would have seen on physical examination. Granted, I didn't shave my legs due to the brand of feminism that was *au courant* on college campuses at that time. In fact, when I had been outside the gynecologist's office, a native-born Italian man had come up to me to say he liked my hairy legs. In Italy, men considered women whose legs were hairy as sexy, and he didn't understand why American women insisted on shaving them. Granted, I had a voice that was deep like Lauren Bacall's and I had been promiscuous, but were these reasons enough for these doctors to order a test to confirm my gender?

"There's nothing I see in the records that would explain to me why they ordered this test," said Dr. Friedman. "And there's nothing I see about you that leads me to even dream of ordering such a test. But I wanted you to know the results, in case you had ever discussed with these doctors any concerns that you had about your gender identity. Did you ever express such concerns to them, or do you have such concerns?"

"I've never thought I was anything but female. I don't remember saying anything that would indicate otherwise. I did tell my mother last year that I was interested in learning to be a carpenter, but she laughed and told me that was only for boys. One time I did ask my father when I was younger if I could use the power mower to mow the lawn, and he said no, it was man's work. Do you think that indicates that I'm confused about my gender?"

Dr. Friedman laughed and raised his eyes to the sky. "No, Linda. Wanting to be a productive member of society is not an indication of gender confusion. You know, my wife is much better at fixing cabinets and using the lawnmower than I am, and I can assure you after 40 years of marriage and three children that she is a woman."

He paused for a moment and looked at me with a broad smile before continuing in a wistful tone, "I was a poor boy from Brooklyn, very poor. No one in my neighborhood ever imagined that I could become a doctor. But that's what I wanted, and I worked during the day and went to high school and college at night to realize my dream. You can realize your dreams, too, if you know what you want and get up again and again whenever you get knocked down."

I probably had about 40 hourly sessions like this with Dr. Friedman during that year. Sometimes I talked with him about my worries over Vietnam, nuclear war and the environment while other times we discussed religion, my family, or my friends both male and female. Much of the time, he simply explained to me things that I didn't understand about my body, mind, or life in general. Dr. Friedman's therapy was a simple recipe of careful listening, compassionate understanding, historical knowledge, creative sensibilities and plain common sense. He was the wise grandfather I'd never had, and I was fortunate indeed that the school psychologist had included him on the list.

THE DEMISE OF DR. SAINZ

WHILE DR. FRIEDMAN EMPLOYED NO DRUGS in treating me—only the listening, information, understanding and insights of talk therapy, there was a clear rise in the influence of the pharmaceutical industry.

Psychiatric practice during the 1950s and '60s is clearly evidenced not only by professional journal articles from that period, but by the ads for medications that are heavily promoted within those journals. How rigorously the reported journal studies were conducted and reviewed, how accurate the findings, and how clear the motives for the research are questions that may never be fully answered. If there were challenges and disputes to the claims made about the benefits of these drugs, they were not made in ways that thwarted their use on patients.

By February 19, 1963, the Utica, New York, *Observer Dispatch* reported about a new research facility at Marcy State Hospital, headed by Dr. Sainz. The article notes, "The hospital's Division of Research has screened and rejected as dangerous dozens of drugs."[62] Despite such cursory acknowledgements of failed drug experiments, few of the journal or newspaper articles describe or question the long-term effects of the medications on the people who received them. No patients, family members, or even non-psychiatric medical professionals are quoted about the effects of the drugs nor polled about their views regarding the therapies.

Nevertheless, within the field of psychiatry during the 1960s, the practice of administering psychotropic drugs to mental patients was coming under increasing criticism. Radical psychiatric therapists such as R.D. Laing and Thomas Szasz questioned the foundations of their profession and offered alternative views about mental illness and health, diagnoses and treatments. Basic questions arose about the manual for diagnosing mental illness, the *Diagnostic and Statistical Manual of Mental Disorders* (DSM). First published in 1952, the year I was born, it would not be revised again until 1968, when I was 16. By the time that the second edition of the DSM was published, it was already being challenged in some medical circles.[63]

During the 1960s, the movement to deinstitutionalize patients in state mental hospitals in the U.S. exploded. The potential to control patients through the use of psychotropic drugs was a key argument made in favor of moving hospital residents back to smaller community halfway houses. In New York State, the population inside state mental hospitals declined dramatically and by 1971, a state-funded consultants' study referred to as "The O'Connor Report" recommended the closing of Marcy State Hospital. This led to a public debate about whether to close the Utica or Marcy Hospital, leaving the future of the Marcy Research Division in question.[64]

These developments may have started Dr. Sainz thinking about leaving New York State at about the same time that I was benefiting from sessions with Dr. Friedman. But a judicial ruling the following year probably clinched that decision.

In October 1972, a man who had been imprisoned in Iowa for 17 years won the chance for a new trial. That man, Ernest Triplett, had confessed to the murder of a child in 1954. But in 1972, a legal appeal on Triplett's behalf uncovered medical records showing that his confession was obtained illegally while under the influence of powerful mind-altering drugs prescribed by Dr. Anthony Sainz at the Cherokee State Hospital in Iowa. It is extremely rare that the public, or even family members, ever get the opportunity to see the medical records of patients in state mental hospitals, so this legal case offers unique insights—beyond my own story—into the psychiatric practice of Anthony Sainz.

Details about the case provide the context within which Ernest Triplett was convicted. In September 1954, the murder of eight-year-old Jimmy Bremmer was front page news in Iowa. The boy had disappeared one evening in late August. Triplett, who had been seen talking to the boy earlier that day, was questioned by local police and released. Soon thereafter, Triplett committed himself for treatment of syphilis to the Cherokee Hospital, where Dr. Anthony Sainz oversaw his care and prescribed his medication.

According to a September 30, 1954 article in the *Lemars Globe Post* in Iowa with the headline, "Jimmy Bremmer Killer May Be Tried in LeMars," Ernest Triplett was a drifter who sold music lessons to children. The article reported that Jimmy Bremmer's decapitated body had been found the day before, and it said that Dr. Sainz had accompanied Triplett when police took this suspect to the wooded spot where the body was found, to observe Triplett's reaction. "By keeping the suspect under the observation of this psychiatrist," the article continues, "the state will avoid the possible raising of the charge that advantage was taken of the suspect's psychiatric condition to induce him to sign a false confession." Later, the article reports, "Triplett underwent two lie detector tests, but the only certain conclusion that seems to have come out of these is that Triplett is definitely a 'queer' [sic]."[65]

What the newspapers did not report in 1954 were details about the treatment Triplett had received under the care of Dr. Anthony Sainz after Triplett had committed himself to the Cherokee Institute. The treatment was not revealed until 18 years later, during Triplett's 1972 legal appeal, when a judge saw the evidence of hospital records and heard the testimony from Dr. Eugene Leander, an expert neuropsychiatrist. Leander told the court that the medical records showed that Sainz had ordered doses of psychoactive drugs to Triplett that "were almost lethal."[66] He was given large amounts of sodium pentothal, desoxyn, seconal and *LSD 25* simultaneously on numerous days prior to his trip to the site where the murdered boy's body was discovered. The potent cognitive effects of these drugs, if it had been known by law enforcement at the time, should have cast extreme doubt on any reaction that Triplett may have displayed there.[67]

About one week later on October 6, 1954, hospital officials extracted a confession from Triplett, just hours after he had been given large doses of mind-altering drugs at separate intervals. The fact that the suspect was under the influence of massive amounts of psychoactive drugs when he confessed was allegedly not revealed to the prosecutor, judge or jury who convicted and sentenced Triplett to life in prison in 1955.

Additional records uncovered in 1972 suggest that Sainz's methods had been questioned by his colleagues at Cherokee in 1954, just as he left that institute to work at a veteran's hospital in another Iowa city.[68] And about one year later, Sainz left that job to conduct research at Marcy State Hospital in New York State. Public accounts indicate that there were no questions about what he did at Cherokee until Ernest Triplett won his appeal 17 years later—17 years that Triplett had spent in a state penitentiary in Iowa for a crime he may not have committed.

Some Iowans argued in 1972 that Triplett was still Jimmy Bremmer's killer and that he got off on a legal technicality. But a nonprofit organization called Iowa Cold Cases points out that, not long after Triplett was in custody and serving time, a little girl named Donna Sue Davis in a nearby community was abducted and killed in a manner similar to that of Jimmy Bremmer. This similar case raises questions about a possible link between the cases that could not be blamed on Triplett.[69]

Donna Sue Davis' killer was never brought to justice.

And neither was Dr. Anthony A. Sainz, who left New York State around 1973 and opened a private psychiatric practice in Lumberton, North Carolina. He would die there in 1979.

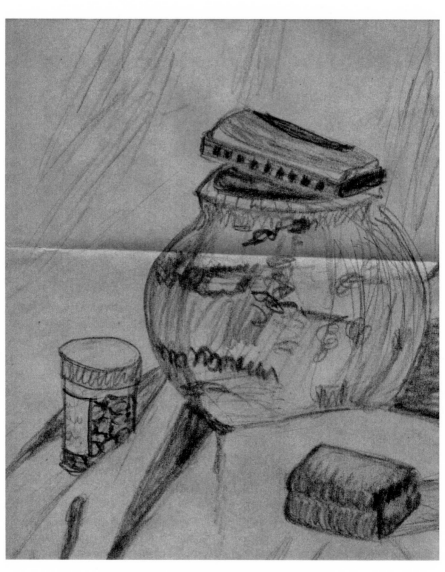

"Pills," by Linda Mary Wagner, 1971.
Sketching was one means to recovery.

"Getting from here to there," by Linda Mary Wagner, 1971.

JOSEPH JOEL FRIEDMAN, M.D., is director of Broome County Community Mental Health Services. In addition, he engages in private practice and serves as consultant in psychiatry and in psychiatric education to the Binghamton (N.Y.) State Hospital.

Starting his career as a platinum jewelry craftsman, Dr. Friedman worked by day and attended Morris Evening High School and then Washington Square Evening College in New York City. He was the first "evening" student to be admitted to University and Bellevue Hospital Medical College, where he received his M.D. in 1934. He interned at Coney Island Hospital, and later served there as assistant visiting pathologist, and at Harbor Hospital as assistant attending surgeon until 1940, when he left to open a private practice in Unadilla, N. Y. He was graduated from the New York School of Psychiatry and in 1959 became a resident at Brooklyn State Hospital. When he left that institution in 1966, he was supervising psychiatrist in charge of the Intensive Therapy Unit.

Dr. Friedman is a diplomate in psychiatry and is certified by The American Board of Medical Hypnosis. He is a fellow of The Academy of Psychosomatic Medicine and a contributing editor of *Psychosomatics*.

From "Contributors to this Issue," *Psychiatric Quarterly*, 1967, Vol. 41, Issue 3

DOCTOR AND SCULPTOR—Dr. Joseph Joel Friedman, commissioner of Broome County Mental Health Services, has been sculpting for a hobby for 30 years. His work will be on display from 2-6 p.m. next Saturday and Sunday at his home at 3245 Dogwood Drive, Binghamton. Proceeds from the exhibit will benefit the Broome Chapter of the Mental Health Association.

From profile of Dr. Joseph Joel Friedman, published in the Binghamton, NY *Sunday Press*, Nov. 12, 1972. The compassionate, attentive care that Dr. Joseph Joel Friedman delivered was a crucial element in Linda's long-term recovery from the trauma inflicted by Dr. Anthony A. Sainz.

IX

NINE LIVES

LIVING ALONE

As the end of the Spring term approached, I knew my grades were strong, my drinking and drug use was minimal and I was more certain of what I wanted from my relationships with men. In addition to Dr. Friedman's care, I was strongly influenced that term by a British professor named Elizabeth Fee, whose History course on Science and Sexuality clarified for me the intellectual underpinnings of "scientific" theories stating that women were inferior to men. She challenged us to take one of these 19th century arguments and counter it with careful and logical arguments in opposition.

I focused on what had passed for scientific evidence that women were inferior because the brains of deceased women, when measured and weighed, were smaller than those of men. I argued first that the author had not controlled for other variables such as aging, trauma, and familial and ethnic differences when measuring and comparing brain sizes. But more centrally, I made the case that even if the brain sizes of women are smaller, bigger is not necessarily better. This point was just beginning to emerge in the area of computing, in which enormous mainframes that had once taken up entire rooms were being replaced by smaller equipment that was more efficient and powerful in capacity. Therefore, it could be easily argued that the smaller size of women's brains may be an indication that they are more fully evolved than those of men.

In addition to this course, the women's consciousness-raising group I had joined provided a good outlet to share my experiences with other female college students. Although it became clear after a time that some in the group were lesbians, most of us were heterosexual. But whether gay or straight, we all shared the experiences of limitations and constraints on our growth and freedom. Just as crucial, nearly all of us had been sexually, physically, or psychologically abused by men who had authority over us, or by boyfriends or acquaintances.

These meetings were revelatory. In a concrete way, I began to see that I was not alone but that I was caught in the same net of oppressive forces with a world of other women. Some told stories of sexual or physical abuse by fathers or uncles, some told of date rapes, sexual harassment by bosses, or psychological bullying by classmates or co-workers. Many of their experiences seemed more horrific and painful than what I went through, but I discovered that they thought the same thing about mine. Together, we were naming and analyzing these forces and in doing so, we were gaining an increasing feeling of control over our own lives.

My roommate June was not involved in this nascent women's movement, and she was not receptive to my suggestions that she join us. She was planning to go home to Brooklyn for the summer, while I needed to take summer classes to catch up on time lost during the fall semester when I dropped out. With my feelings of self-confidence blooming, I decided that I wanted to live alone, to prove to myself that I could live independently. I found a spacious one-bedroom flat on a second floor with plenty of windows, not far from a bus stop. After finals were done, I packed up and moved with help from some friends.

With fabrics that my mother let me take from home, I made seat covers and curtains and found used furniture at tag sales. I scrubbed the floors, sinks, refrigerator and cupboards and stocked the shelves with things that I preferred to eat. I decided to go cold turkey on sugar—eating a diet rich in fresh vegetables, whole grains and fruits that was close to what was then called "macrobiotic."

I found great pleasure in living alone and relished my autonomy, privacy and freedom. I was able to decorate in whatever way I chose, have friends over whenever I wanted, and best of all, I was able to bring a beautiful black kitten into my life. I named her Deirdre, after a tragic figure in Irish mythology.

I continued to see Dr. Friedman, but I gradually went less and less frequently. I enjoyed my classes, had a housecleaning job to earn some cash, and had started running and swimming for fitness. I had short-term involvements with a number of men, but they all left me yearning for a more meaningful, substantial love relationship and real sexual satisfaction.

During the month of June that year, there was a severe rainstorm that lasted several days. It resulted in some of the most severe flooding ever experienced in the southern tier of New York State. At some point during the follow-up news coverage, I saw an article that pointed out that during the previous 365 days in the Binghamton area, there were fewer than 40 days that had even partial sunshine. They say that people in Seattle don't grow old, they rust. Well, Binghamton had been second only to Seattle in the amount of rain and cloudy days.

Early in the fall semester, I learned that I could spend a semester at another State University of New York campus with no additional cost and with full acceptance of any credits at either school. I applied for this semester away at the Buffalo campus.

In those years, Buffalo was considered "the Berkeley of the East" because of its political climate. And while it had far more snow than Binghamton, it also had more sunshine. At the end of the term, I packed up again and moved to Buffalo.

Shortly before I left, I had a dream so vivid, I can still see, hear and feel it today. I was lying down in my bed in my dream, and Dr. Friedman was sitting at my side. He said, "You'll be fine very soon." And suddenly I heard beautiful music and the man sitting next to my bed was no longer Dr. Friedman, but a much younger man. I awoke with the music still playing in my head and more questions than answers.

SHUFFLE OFF TO BUFFALO

"I feel like this is the beginning
Though I've known you for a million years."

– "You Are the Sunshine of My Life"
Stevie Wonder 1973

BUFFALO CAME WITH A READY-MADE LIVING arrangement. My old friend Anne was going to school there and she had already found a three-bedroom apartment right next to the main campus and had lined up another roommate. She asked me to move in with them and I agreed, very happy I didn't have to search for a place to live.

While I had enjoyed living alone for the previous seven months, late in my stay there I had encountered a nasty stomach illness that landed me in the college infirmary for a week. This experience convinced me that I preferred to share my life and living quarters and to have a support network at home. With Anne and Patty, this support was immediate. We got along well, shared our painful pasts, acted silly and laughed together, and cooked and ate together often.

Since Anne had been in Buffalo for the previous two years, she had a group of friends established and I was invited to join them for dinner, parties and hanging around on campus. At a birthday party for one of her friends from Long Island, I met a dark-haired, bearded young man named Barry, who had a nice smile and a contagious laugh. He had also just arrived in Buffalo as a transfer from a private upstate college who had dropped out the previous term and was now re-entering school. We had a good conversation and went our separate ways after the party.

By chance, Barry and I both had landed work-study jobs at the student center Rathskeller cafeteria and sometimes our shifts overlapped. We began developing a friendship. Then in mid-February, the Brazilian students on campus held an evening Carnaval celebration, with live Brazilian music and a lot of dancing. I dressed up for the occasion and went to the event, hoping to connect with a dancing partner there. Before long, I ran into Barry and pulled him onto the dance floor. Unknown to me, he had arranged to meet another young woman at the dance, but she never showed up. We danced throughout the evening, laughed and sang with the band. And when the Carnaval was over, I asked, "My place or yours?"

His roommates were away, and so he asked me to his apartment. We talked, listened to some music, took a shower and slept together that night. In the morning, I was surprised to feel unusual contentment after what I thought might be a one-night stand. My mind was clear, my heart was full, my body felt satisfied, and I was looking forward to the future. He walked me to my apartment and when we parted, we made plans to see each other again.

Barry had been surviving on a case of tomato soup, and our place always had brown rice, vegetables and sometimes even some meat for dinner. While I'm sure the food was part of the appeal of hanging around our apartment, I know that our mutual desire and affection was the primary attraction. We had plenty of interests in common: we ran and played chess together, shared similar political views, and I loved his taste in music.

One afternoon, he brought a gift with him. By the size and shape, I could tell it was an LP—that is, one of the large vinyl recordings of that era. While I expected it might be Stevie Wonder, the Grateful Dead or Joni Mitchell—all of them favorites—it was Rimsky-Korsakov's *Rite of Spring*. Just as with Scheherazade a few years earlier, I did not know this symphony by name. He put the album on the stereo and the music filled the room. I listened, enraptured by the sound.

"This is the music!" I shouted. "This is the music that was in my dream."

"What dream?" he asked.

"Just before I left Binghamton, I had a dream where my doctor said, 'You'll be fine soon.' And this music—this same symphony you just put on the stereo—was playing in the background. And then in the dream, Dr. Friedman transformed into a younger man." I looked at Barry, puzzled, surprised and amazed at this realization.

The more I got to know him, the deeper my feelings for him grew. His older brother had had polio; my older sister had had spinal meningitis. His parents were poor kids from Brooklyn; mine were poor kids from upstate. He had a traumatic experience in college; I had a traumatic experience in my last year in high school. The stories of our lives poured out to each other.

For the first time in my life, I felt entirely connected with a man as a friend, a lover and a companion.

And yet, I would almost lose it all through another close call yet to come.

SPRING BREAK

ANNE WAS ALWAYS READY FOR ADVENTURE. Our spring break was coming and she suggested that we go to Daytona Beach, Florida, for a vacation from the Buffalo winter. Since we didn't have the money for a plane or bus, she suggested that we hitchhike.

Hitchhiking was not uncommon for college students in those years. I had hitched from Rome to Ithaca when I was in high school, from Binghamton to Long Island and from Rochester and Albany while in college. I hitched around Buffalo frequently, and other than a few suggestive comments from some male drivers, I never had any trouble.

So the idea of hitching to Florida excited me. I told Barry, and he expressed no concerns, although he told me later that he was worried about it. I called my parents to tell them my plans and while they were quiet, they didn't argue or tell me not to go. By that time, I was 19 years old, and I suppose they had given up on giving me advice. They just said, "Be careful and have a good time."

The trip started out well. With our road atlas and calculations of the best routes to take, the trip was approximately 1,200 miles or about 20 hours—depending on the destinations of the drivers who would pick us up. These were the years long before Google maps, and the highways available were vintage 1972. On the side of Route 90 just south of Buffalo where a friend had dropped us off, Anne and I sat on our backpacks and talked.

"Anne, I think I'm in love."

"With Barry?" she asked.

"Yes. I've never felt this way about anyone before. I mean, I thought I loved Tom and Paul, but this is so much richer and deeper and more meaningful than any relationship I've ever had."

"I thought you might be feeling that way about him. I think it's wonderful. You seem so happy!"

Just then, a car pulled over. It was a young man who was headed home to rural southern Pennsylvania, so we hopped in the car. We had a great time talking with him, and he invited us into his parents' home. His mother had just baked an apple pie and urged us to come in for pie and coffee. We graciously accepted and when we left, his mother told us to take care of ourselves and be wary of strangers, even though they had been strangers.

Her son drove us back to a convenient spot on the highway, and we stuck out our thumbs again. During the next part of the journey, we rode a long distance with two middle-aged white men. After we refused to grant them sexual favors, they dropped us off in the mountains of Jefferson National Forest in the middle of the night. Luckily, it was not too long before a tractor-trailer came along and once again, the driver was headed in our direction to Jacksonville, Florida, only about 90 miles away from our Daytona Beach destination.

He left us off on the highway near Jacksonville and within another hour, two young men pulled over to pick us up. They asked us where we were going and when we said, "Daytona Beach," they said they were headed there, too. They looked about our age, and seemed to have friendly faces and voices. The driver wore sunglasses, a military style haircut, and seemed reserved.

His friend, in the front passenger seat, was a bit chubby, with a big smile, an Afro and a Florida State University T-shirt. Since they were African-American, we felt it would be racist to turn down their offer of a ride. Anne and I both climbed into the back seat, not thinking twice about the fact that it was a two-door car.

We chatted for a while with the guy in the passenger seat, but the driver was very quiet. Within about five miles, the driver took an exit off the highway and we were soon on a rural road, surrounded by tall crops. Anne and I looked at each other, both of us feeling the same alarm at the same moment. I said, "Where are you going?" my voice noticeably filled with anxiety.

Now both men were silent. Anne pointed to the side of the car—in a two-door car, there is no way for people in the back seat to escape. They continued to drive for about another ten minutes until they pulled down a dirt road that was as isolated as any I had ever seen and stopped the car.

Once again, I was four years old, trapped inside a dark, hot, locked place. I started to hear in my head, "Row, row, row your boat gently down the stream. Merrily, merrily, merrily, merrily, life is but a dream…"

The driver turned around and showed us a gun. "If you just do as we say, no one will get hurt." He pointed to Anne. "You stay here with me." He pointed to me. "You go with my friend here."

The man in the passenger seat got out of the car, and held the seat back so that both of us could get out. I said to Anne in a whisper, "Do you think we should try to run?"

She said, "He has a gun. I think we should just go along with them."

I was with the younger of the two and as Anne and the other man disappeared into the distance, he put his arm around me and walked with me away from the car. He told me he just wanted to have some fun, and that I should just relax and enjoy myself.

Certain that this was going to be the place where my life ended, after I had finally found the love of my life, all I could think about was how stupid it was to get into the back seat of a two-door car. Time slowed to a crawl. Every breath I took was amplified, every step I took was as loud as a door slamming, and every birdcall was like a scream. I looked up and I could read my obituary in the sky.

This college-age young man engaged in what he thought was foreplay, and then raped me. When he was done, he helped me back to my feet and asked me if I had enjoyed it. I lied and said yes, afraid that I might anger him and further endanger myself otherwise. This is not an uncommon response for a rape victim, who fears for her life, to give to her rapist. In fact, it may be one source of the faulty argument that rapists make, "She wanted it; she was asking for it."

And then, as we walked back toward the car, he said, "You should be careful hitchhiking in Florida, sweetheart. The cops might pick you up because it's illegal." The irony of what he said rang in my ears, while it totally escaped him.

His partner had finished with Anne and they were standing next to the car. I was utterly relieved to see Anne still alive, since she was with the man who had the gun. She and I exchanged silent, knowing looks of terror, realizing that he still had the weapon in this isolated farm field, and now they had already gotten what they wanted from us. I felt my last breath squeezed out of my lungs, if only in my imagination.

But then the driver said, "Get in, we'll drive you back to the highway. First, give me your cash." We handed over the money we had left, and got into the back seat again. They did, in fact, drive us back to the highway and left us by the side of the road where they had picked us up. As soon as we got out and they drove away, I burst into tears. Anne, in contrast, laughed hysterically, as she often did under duress.

It was late afternoon and traffic was heavy. Anne and I decided that, from there onward, we'd take rides only from tractor-trailer drivers who were on the job, and that we'd pretend that we were lesbians. We debated about where to go and decided we'd still head toward Daytona Beach. Soon a truck pulled over and we climbed in. He was going past Daytona, so we were in luck.

It was early evening by the time we got to Daytona, and we had only a few dollars that we had hidden in our packs before we left. We met a couple of young guys who said they could help us out with a place to stay. They were living in a nice house and seemed to have money. I stayed with one of them and Anne with the other. When I got to his room, he tried to impress me with a cache of weapons there. By that time, all I could do was laugh. I simply thought, if I'm toast, I'm toast. I'm too exhausted to put up a fight. But the weapons turned out to be just for show. I woke up in the morning alive, rested and well. We all had breakfast, and then I called my parents to let them know I had been robbed and needed them to wire me some money.

My older siblings say that my parents were distraught at the sound of my voice, which must have betrayed my desperation and fear. But they never let on during the call. They listened, told me they were just glad to hear from me, and quickly wired me some funds that enabled us to get back to Buffalo by bus.

CENTERED WITH CLOSURE

In some sense, I had died in that Florida field, just as I had died after my parents met Anthony Sainz, or when I took my backpack and razor blades out to the campus roadside at Harpur College, or when I came to the conclusion that I just could not and did not believe in the dogma of the Catholic Church. Life, for me, had become a series of traumatic endings to the person I had once been.

On my journey back from Florida to Buffalo, I placed new limits on the risks I was willing to take, and made crucial decisions about what I wanted most from life. The first thing that crystallized was my desire for a long-term meaningful love relationship, and I was convinced that Barry was the right match for me. When I saw him again, the story of the rape poured out from me, but in an odd, calm monotone. The hitchhiking adventure may have seemed as only one more close call that I had survived but this was the one that centered me, that enabled me to sail my boat calmly, even in the worst waters.

Close calls will do that.

Luckily, Barry felt the same way about me and that spring, we began a life together that we still share with great happiness and gratitude.

The vignettes of my brushes with near death and psychological destruction pale in comparison with the great historical forces of violence, war and revolution in the years just prior to my birth in 1952 and the years of my childhood and adolescence. The salves of time and distance have soothed the anger, pain and fear that had obscured my vision of the past for many years, and it's not clear whether my stories have much meaning outside the context of the historical forces at work during my life.

I was left wondering for years what the damage was from these events and was it permanent? I needed to know, what can I still fix? And when I see children—my own and others—tumble into one trouble or another, I wonder how can the damaged goods inside me be a useful lesson to them, and to their parents? Could anything that happened to me prevent the pain and heartache that they might suffer?

Now when I look back at the locked trunk, the drop on the head, the fainting game, the chemical lobotomy, the suicide attempt and the rape, I see clearly the alternate ending for each episode. Over time, it has occurred to me that each close brush with death is, in fact, a small death; each phase of one's life ends in grief and mourning for the self you have grown beyond. Each ending leads to a new phase with the birth of a new identity, a type of reincarnation of one's spirit in a new physical environment, if not an entirely new body.

This leads me to believe that death itself, as the physical end of an individual human life, is entry to a new adventure—with all the excitement and promise of the unknown. It is taken with a leap of faith that something sweeter, kinder and more beautiful is on the other side, at the same time knowing that there will also be struggle, pain and sorrow in the passage.

Somehow, it appears to me now that this cycle will never end, and we cannot know at this stage within our human existence how our being will shift into another dimension that we cannot see from our vantage point here on earth. But I've grown more convinced over the years that our new form is reflected in the billions of stars we see in the sky. As those stars blow up, burn out and disappear, or race across the sky trailing a meteor tail, they are simply suffering another small death that leads to some type of new beginning that we cannot yet fathom.

CLOSURE

It has taken me nearly 40 years to surmise that I have suffered for decades from post-traumatic stress disorder. I started to write this memoir after I had been working in crisis communications for many years and decided that this line of work was unhealthy for me, and that I could not stand to do it one day longer. I accepted a nearly 35% cut in salary to move along in my life, into a new area of work—nonprofit leadership in the health sector. During my free time, I worked on my memoir, trying to figure out why I seemed addicted to imagining disaster around every corner, which both fortunately and unfortunately, makes one very good at crisis planning.

Those questions—why do I have these antennae for catastrophe and the resulting fight-or-flight reactions, and how can I stop it—convinced me to take the time and energy to tell this story and to try to figure out a central mystery in my life—who in the world was Dr. Anthony Sainz and why did he do what he did to me?

My healing did not end in 1973 when I met Barry, or in 1979, the year that Barry and I were married and Dr. Sainz died. Even the five years I have spent writing, researching and editing this manuscript will not end the disorder completely, although it has certainly helped me to put it into perspective. Anxiety seems hard-wired into my brain, and that may have been true at birth.

But my experience at age 17 with Dr. Sainz, like my experience as a four-year-old trapped in a clothes trunk in an attic, have amplified and focused my fears. I wanted to turn these experiences into something useful.

In the course of my research, I read Robert Whitaker's *Mad in America* and *Anatomy of an Epidemic*, and I realized more clearly than I had previously that my story does not belong to me alone. It is a story that touches upon thousands of people who have found themselves caught within a labyrinth of mental health treatments that can be very difficult to escape, even when you have recovered, even if you were never truly mentally ill at all.

Literary agents have told me that my story is not unique, it's just another wrinkle of *Girl Interrupted*, or *One Flew Over the Cuckoo's Nest*. But what have those tales done to change the way we treat people with emotional and mental distress? Sometimes, the same old story must be told again and again. I tell the tale with wrinkles that make it mine, because the fundamentals of this story affect so many patients and their families and friends, and we must stop going down blind alleys about mental health.

I am fortunate that I reached closure and peace with my father before his brain succumbed to Alzheimer's disease, a physiologically based mental illness that researchers still struggle to understand. I am grateful that I finally comprehend how my mother, a devout Catholic with memories of her ill sister Leona imprinted deeply in her mind, would have so readily believed in a doctor recommended by a priest when she feared that her daughter was following in her sister's footsteps.

I appreciate the chance to look back on the late 1960s when I was in high school, amazed that I and so many other baby boomers survived with our lives and any sanity intact, because the entire society had turned upside-down and we all seemed to be living in Alice's Wonderland.

My parents were right in thinking that I needed help. What they didn't understand was that I needed them to turn off the TV and see the real person, me, sitting in front of them. I needed them to talk to my friends' parents and come to watch me cheerlead at school games. I needed my mother to give me a full bear hug. I needed them both to admit to me how confused the entire world had become to them, to tell me stories from their own young lives and describe how they surmounted the challenges they had faced. And I needed them to question authority.

But these were not skills my mom or dad had learned at home or at school. They finished high school at the age of 16 and were thrown into the Great Depression. They had few options, and life to them had no shades of gray, but was filled with only black and white.

After I went off to college, the television show *Phil Donahue* taught my mother about many things she had never learned before—that women could enjoy sex, that you can be Catholic and question what a priest says, and that children need their mother to express physical affection and say the words, "I love you." The first time I visited my parents after my mother heard me on the radio as a reporter on NPR, she embraced me in a way she never had before. I want to believe that this is because she finally realized that I had overcome her fears about me. I had succeeded in my life in a way that she could understand, a way that her sister never could.

In the long run, it was my mother who paid a steeper price for blind faith in the medical profession. A doctor mistakenly doubled the dosage of her blood thinner after implanting a pacemaker she probably never needed in the first place. The result was one hemorrhagic stroke that sent her to the hospital, where a young resident made another error that caused a second bleeding in her brain, and left her right side paralyzed and her mind struggling to form and find words. My mother spent the last 17 years of her life in a nursing home, completely incontinent, unable to feed herself, unable to speak. The pain of seeing my parents in this condition at the end of their lives was another, different type of trauma.

I have been the lucky one in this family saga. I survived Dr. Sainz and I am able to tell the tale that needs to be heard and heeded. There was some hidden inner love that my parents gave to me that enabled me to pull through it and because of my concern for them, I gave up on suicide as a solution. But at least as important to my survival, there was overt help I received from Carol and Marilyn, and acts of kindness from Chris, Anne, Bonne, my other sisters and my brother, my little nieces and nephews, and my many friends and classmates.

There was the amazing gift of Dr. Joseph Joel Friedman, and several other truly good psychologists who helped me confront the ghosts of Aunt Leona and Dr. Sainz at various points in my adult life. These include Jim Iberg, who introduced me to the Focusing technique of psychotherapy and helped me see my own value, and Mary Hendricks, who found the right moment to tell me, "It's OK if things aren't perfect." There was the psychologist in Hastings-on-Hudson who told me that most of his patients had far less trauma in their histories and that I was incredibly well-adjusted considering what I had experienced.

And throughout the many years since these traumas, there has been my lover/husband Barry and ultimately my own dearest children, whose deep care and concern, words of encouragement, and demonstrations of physical affection have lifted me up time and again. When that dark specter in the attic has reared its ugly head, they have been there reminding me to believe in myself.

Sometimes these family members, friends and colleagues tell me things I do not want to hear, but that is what mental health requires. Tragedies of the past need not be repeated if you have the honest support of friends and family, and if you find a way to develop faith in yourself. The past need not be prologue if you face the truth.

Finding the love of her life and an anchor of emotional support in Barry
Ginsberg was another critical piece of Linda's recovery.

EPILOGUE

"You look just the same…"

ALTHOUGH I WAS MUCH HEAVIER AT my 40th high-school reunion than the last time I'd seen them, my Rome Catholic High School classmates who were there saw the same person in me that they remembered. My smile and large nose were as distinctive as they had ever been. Several people told my husband that I was "the smart one," or "She was always efficient," but no one asked, "So what was really wrong with you in the middle of senior year?" To me it was amazing, having spent the previous three years writing this book, that no one would mention the period during January 1970 when I disappeared from school, after which I must have seemed like a zombie.

Instead, everyone spoke only of the better days of the external me. In contrast, when a few reunion attendees stepped forward to tell funny or happy remembrances, I could recall clearly the painful time of feeling as if I was "persona non grata." I was remembering only the internal me during my most difficult months.

When I mentioned that I was working on this memoir, the word spread throughout the crowd and many voices said, "I want to read that!" Immediately I realized that each one of them could have figured into a happier recollection of my high school years:

complete with tales of football and basketball games, rolling up our skirts when the priests and nuns weren't looking, secret food fights in the cafeteria, getting drunk at senior prom, and arguing points of history, literature, or religion in classrooms and hallways. There were robust harmonies in chorus, heartfelt scenes in class plays, belly laughs at sleepovers, and dreams shared while gazing at the sky from the shores of Lake Delta.

To everyone in my high-school class, I'm sorry that this tale could not include each of you. But I know that you were all a major influence that helped me survive my senior year and the painful recovery that followed. We lived together through our most impressionable youthful years during one of history's crazier epochs. At the reunion, we had a lot of laughs and fond recollections, while sharing recent common experiences of empty nests and failing parents. We acknowledged the four from the Class of 1970 who had passed away—one from colon cancer, others from breast cancer, leukemia, or aneurysm. Since then we've heard of other losses to massive heart attacks. And we wondered whether the classmates whose addresses we had not been able to find were still alive and well.

What became clear to me from this reunion is that no one and nothing turned out quite as we might have predicted. Some of those with the most open hearts and smiles as teens now seem embittered or harsh. One quiet, handsome boy has become a beautiful, gay male dancer. A friend who thought she'd die like her mom did at the age of 50 is still alive, strong and cancer-free past 60. Kids who kept an insecure low profile have blossomed into assertive, successful salespeople, while some of the most visible, including me, have grown more introspective and reserved with age.

I hesitate to say that Shakespeare was wrong, but in my book, my past has not been my prologue. I believe that no one should doom themselves, their children and certainly not their patients, to a life of despair and fear. I believe that a psychiatrist should always second-guess his diagnosis, and ensure that his or her assessment of a patient is checked by at least one other mental health professional. I believe that we must, as a society, pursue physical and mental health, rather than simply treating what we view as mental and physical illness.

And medical researchers of all stripes should strive to identify the physiological roots of what is glibly called "insanity" or "mental illness." History has shown us too many people were warehoused as "crazy" when they actually had tuberculosis, syphilis, Alzheimer's disease, thyroid disease, or even simple poverty.

To my RCH classmates, my old friends, my siblings, and the many good doctors I've met, I am eternally grateful that your support helped me bridge from troubled waters to a calmer, happier future.

As far as our system of mental health care, I will let some others speak.

On the New York Traveler website that showcases photos of the Utica Lunatic Asylum buildings, a visitor writes:

§Beth on Tue, 9th Aug 2011 5:07 pm

I would like to extend my heartfelt empathy to those who know the mental health system via necessity. I would like to offer a bit of solace, as well as a plea, to recognize that the care of mental illness has run the gamut...from hushed stigma to outrageous therapies, from ignorant shame to informed hope. There is reason for optimism with today's therapies and pharmacological advances. Nevertheless, as a society we will always bear the stain of inadequate care, even atrocities, put upon our most vulnerable citizens. Those most deserving of kindness and compassion were greeted with isolation and ill-informed guesswork in what passed for treatment. However, it is not accurate to believe that no good ever came to the afflicted inhabitants of Utica Psychiatric Center. There are, indeed, countless stories of lives restored, workers whose dedication was a thriving example of professionalism, and people who were discharged with a fighting chance to gain re-entry to fulfilling and productive lives. Yes, there were valiant efforts with a righteous goal, but far more is waiting to be accomplished. This building is not a symbol of shame, just a stoic and cavernous shell that tells the story of our culture's tortured journey in the treatment of mental illness. The system failed then because it didn't understand the disease. Now, despite all we know, we continue to risk failure seemingly because we do not learn from history...Perhaps this is the real majesty, and travesty, of Old Main: she stands alone in her decomposing grandeur. While many gape at her beauty and marvel at her storied past, most walk or drive by on a daily basis, barely noticing her as she stands in silence. Not unlike how we continue to see mental illness.

Dozens of New York residents, like my siblings and me, have been eager to gain access to historical records regarding their relatives who were institutionalized at these facilities, but state law in New York and most other states makes that impossible.

While the historic facilities with politically incorrect names haunt our collective unconscious, the current name for such treatment centers seems more sanitized, if not exactly compassionate. For example, the Central New York Psychiatric Center seems less obtrusive while some former asylums have been re-purposed as prisons. In "History of the Town of Marcy" by

Ray Ball at The Town of Marcy website, Marcy State Hospital is described:

> From Hospital to Prison
>
> Just as Marcy farmers are slowly disappearing from the scene, the same thing happened at Marcy State Hospital, where in 1961 it was found that produce could be purchased cheaper than it could be grown. This resulted in the closing of the farm colony. It was also a signal of changes that would soon happen in the care of the mentally ill. Improved medicines and the need to reduce costs led to discharging more patients to outside care. Soon both Utica and Marcy State Hospitals would be almost totally closed, affecting the employment of Marcy area residents. In the 1980's a new era began, making use of the former hospital buildings by converting them into prisons. This activity has grown so extensively that another prison was soon built on the grounds once used by the farm colony.[70]

As the ghosts of Aunt Leona and Dr. Sainz can attest, the history of the treatment of mental illness in the United States and around the world is stuffed with horrors and sprinkled with some successes. The most well-meaning families, doctors and researchers have been stymied by the mysteries of the human mind. These obscure findings have resulted in well-intentioned cruelties, misunderstandings, and physical and emotional harm to those who strike the majority as insane, irrational, or out of control.

Finding the gems of beneficial treatment and separating them from the warehousing—whether we have caged people in straightjackets, lobotomies, electroshock, or pharmaceuticals—is one of the greatest challenges of our time. The diagnoses of mental illness in the U.S. alone are climbing dramatically, while the rate of those who end up as permanently disabled has reached epidemic proportions, as laid out in Robert Whitaker's book, *The Anatomy of an Epidemic*.

We have another chance to think outside the box—outside that attic trunk in which I was locked, outside the almshouses, electroshocks, Utica Asylums, lobotomies, Cherokee Institutes, forced-labor farms, Willard State Hospitals, pharmaceutical straightjackets and half-hearted Halfway Houses.

The mentally ill are our mothers, fathers, sisters, brothers, sons and daughters, aunts and uncles. We cannot hide them from us. They are us. They—and we—need our kindest, most honest, compassionate and caring selves to cope with the trials we all face in being human.

The family of Fred & Eleanor Wagner (seated) at their 50th wedding anniversary party.
Standing, from left: Joan, Carol, Betty, Richard, Linda, Diane.

Linda's parents, Fred and Eleanor Wagner, at left in about 1974.
On the right, they are shown in 1990 at the nursing home where they lived out their final years.

Rest in peace–Frederick Ernest Wagner, 1913–1992.
Eleanor Port Wagner, 1913–2006.

Willard State Hospital in its early days of 'moral treatment.'

"Whatever comes to pass, it is to be hoped that the spirit of Willard as set forth in the first report of the Trustees will continue. It would be a home 'for those people who have neither home nor friends and who are without the means financially or the capacity intellectually to provide for themselves, with the intellect shattered, minds darkened, living amid delusions, constant prey to unrest, haunted by unreal fantasies and wild imagining. They now have, in their sore misfortune, a safe refuge, kindly care, constant watching and are as comfortable as their circumstances will allow.'"[71]

History of Willard Asylum for the Insane
and the Willard State Hospital
by Robert E. Doran, M.D.

AFTERWORD

SINCE SOME BOOKS SOLD AS MEMOIR have resulted in controversy about their truth, let me clarify what you can and cannot rely on in this account as factual. The events in this book actually happened to me or around me—you need not doubt that they happened and that they are part of my personal experience. The description of events that happened to other people may not be precisely accurate, but they are as I recall them, or as I have documented them through research.

I have taken some poetic license with the use of the term "mystery" in my subtitle, since the publishing world views mystery as a fiction genre, and this memoir is non-fiction. I use the word because this book is the result of my efforts to solve the mysteries surrounding my encounters with a psychiatrist at ages 17-18. Through a process of discovery that unfolded over many decades, I have solved that mystery to my satisfaction. But I have uncovered other mysteries, some of which I cannot address without greater investigative resources, and some of which it's doubtful that anyone could ever solve.

Some detail and dialogue in the telling of these events involves an amalgam of details that I remember over a period of time in my childhood. I cannot testify under oath that, for example, the soap opera that my mother was watching was "As the World Turns" versus "The Secret Storm." But I can testify that my mother frequently watched both of these shows and called them "my stories" while she stood starching and ironing my father's shirts as impeccably as any professional laundry I've ever paid.

In the case of personal friends, I have either avoided last names or changed them to protect their privacy. With regard to the personal histories of family members, friends, or the physicians whom I encountered during my late teens and early 20s, I have done my best to base these on documentary research and oral histories. According to St. Elizabeth's Hospital in Utica, New York, my own medical records were destroyed in the 1990s as a matter of routine procedure, many years before I began writing this book.

Regarding some of the general history about the treatment of the mentally ill in our country, I wish to credit Richard Whitaker, author of *Mad in America* and *Anatomy of an Epidemic*. Whitaker is an excellent journalist who has devoted significant time and energy, along with detailed and thorough research, into an aspect of our society's past and present that we have shamefully ignored to the detriment of many American families.

Whitaker also documents treatments that have contributed to mental health for those deemed mentally ill. His research supports my own personal finding—that the tragedies of the past need not be repeated if we provide love and support to our family and friends, and encourage those who are troubled to find faith in themselves.

My memories of my childhood and young adulthood bleed into each other. What is clearest and truest about them are the feelings they evoke in me to this day.

Despite the pain among those feelings, I have unearthed the ghosts that have haunted me for 40 years, stared them in the face, and laid them to their final resting place in this book.

NOTES

ENDNOTES

1 Susan Krauss Whitbourne, "Fulfillment at Any Age – Mindlessness and Memory Slips: How to Find What You've Lost," *Psychology Today Online* January 25, 2011, September 4, 2013 www.psychologytoday.com.

2 "This Godless Communism," (*Treasure Chest of Fun & Fact*, 1961). *Treasure Chest of Fun & Fact* was a Catholic comic book published by George A. Pflaum. Archives of the Catholic University of America. September 3, 2013 http://archives.lib.cua.edu/findingaid/treasurechest.cfm. The series, with years until 1964 in the public domain, can be found online at http://www.aladin0.wrlc.org/gsdl/collect/treasure/treasure.shtml.

3 David L. Lightner, *Asylum, Prison and Poorhouse: The Writings and Reform Work of Dorothea Dix in Illinois* (Carbondale Edwardsville, Southern Illinois University Press, 1999).

4 Information about Dorothy Dix from the following sites: *The Social Welfare History Project* on Dorothea Lynde Dix at http://www.Socialwelfarehistory.com. Muskinghum College, New Concord, Ohio, History of Psychology Archives at http://www.muskingum.edu/~psych/psycweb/history/dix.htm and "Dorothea Dix, Philanthropist," Review of Life of Dorothea Lynde Dix, (*New York Times*, October 20, 1890.)

5 Robert E. Doran, "History of Willard Asylum for the Insane and the Willard State Hospital" (1978,

Original paper housed at New York State Library), 5-9.

6 Doran, p. 9.

7 Doran, p. 21.

8 Metrazol: "The use of Metrazol as a convulsive agent was discovered by the Hungarian-American neurologist and psychiatrist Ladislas J. Meduna in 1934. It works by inhibiting action of GABA, the chief inhibitory neurotransmitter in mammals to induce convulsions. Meduna was interested in treating schizophrenia and had made an observation that patients that died with epilepsy had more brain glia than patients with schizophrenia. He theorized that by inducing seizures in patients suffering from schizophrenia that it would increase the presence of glia and reverse the mental illness. From the Web Site of Fairfield State Hospital website, Fairfield, Connecticut, September 2, 2013 http://www.fairfieldstatehospital.com/metrazol.html.

9 Doran, p. 25.

10 Doran, p. 40.

11 Darby Penney and Peter Stastny. *The Lives They Left Behind: Suitcases from a State Hospital Attic*, (Belleview Literary Press, New York, 2008) September 2, 2013 http://www.suitcaseexhibit.org/indexhasflash.html.

12 James R. Wagner. "Wagner and Allied Families Scrapbook," family genealogical paper, (1998) 5-30.

13 Information taken from the following speeches by Dr. Sainz. "Dr. Sainz to Talk at County Public Health Dinner," *The Laurens Sun*, Laurens, Iowa April 22, 1954: 1; "Iowa City Man in Talk Monday at Cedar Falls," *Waterloo Daily Courier*, March 4, 1955: 17; "Mental Health Conclave Set," *Evening Recorder*, Amsterdam, New York, April 19, 1958.

14 "Contributors to this issue: Anthony Sainz, M.D.," *Psychiatric Quarterly* 31, Numbers 1-4 (January 1957) 190-197.

15 Victor W. Sidel. "Herbert Abrams in China: International Social Medicine, Journal of Public Health Policy (2007) 28, 167.

16 "Agreement for UNRRA." *Pillars of Peace: Documents Pertaining To American Interest In Establishing A Lasting World Peace.* (1946): *Ibiblio.* Web. September 3, 2013 http://www.ibiblio.org/pha/policy/1943/431109a.html.

17 "Famed Medic of Cherokee To Talk Here," *The Emmetsburg Democrat* March 19 1953: 1.

18 "Dr. Sainz to Talk at County Public Health Dinner," *The Laurens Sun* [Laurens, Iowa] 22 April 1954: 1.

19 Email correspondence between author and Roxane *(sic)* Moller, Cherokee Mental Health Institute, Iowa Department of Human Services, February 17, 2009.

20 Bob Cudmore. "Life in 1946," *The Daily Gazette.* June 20, 2009.

21 The Adirondacks are a northern New York State mountain range.

22 City of Rome, NY History. September 2, 2013 http://www.Romenewyork.com.

23 Rome, NY military history museum. September 5, 2013 http://romemilitary-museum.tripod.com/.

24 "The Old Main, or Utica Lunatic Asylum, NY," September 2, 2013 http://newyorktraveler.net/the-old-main-or-utica-lunatic-asylum-ny/.

25 The Doors. "Break on Through (To the Other Side)," *The Doors.* Elektra Records, 1967. Vinyl.

26 "Just War Doctrine," *Catholic Answers to Explain and Defend the Faith* September 5, 2013 http://www.catholic.com/documents/just-war-doctrine.

27 Thomas C. Fox, "Vietnam's 400-year Catholic History," *National Catholic Reporter*, April 24, 2003. September 5, 2013   http://www.nationalcatholicreporter.org/todaystake/tt042403.htm.

28 "Dr. Wynegar To Leave Mental Health Institute," *Cedar Rapids Gazette*, Cedar Rapids, Iowa, July 25, 1952: 11.

29 "Public Invited on Tour of Cherokee State Hospital," *Le Mars Semi Weekly Sentinel* [Le Mars, Iowa] May 29, 1951: 2.

30 "Iowa City Man in Talk Monday at Cedar Falls," Waterloo Daily Courier, March 4, 1955: 17; "Teachers Meet Here Wednesday," Oelwein Daily Register, Oelwein, Iowa, October 30, 1954: 8; "Mental Health Conclave Set," Evening Recorder, Amsterdam, New York, April 19, 1958.

31 "Brain Surgery Is Performed at State Institute," *Cedar Rapids Gazette*, March 13, 1953: 15.

32 "The Lobotomist" documentary was broadcast as part of The American Experience on PBS in 2008. http://www.pbs.org/wgbh/americanexperience/films/lobotomist/player/. Accessed September 5, 2013. Historic footage of actual lobotomies being performed can be viewed in an excerpt from the documentary at http://www.youtube.com/watch?v=_0aNILW6Ilk

33 Walter Freeman "Amygdaloidectomy for the suppression of auditory hallucinations; a preliminary report of a theory and its application in one case," *Medical Annals of the District of Columbia*, 1951.

34 "Open Large-scale Surgery on State Mental Patients," *Council Bluffs Iowa Nonpareil*, July 20, 1952: 24.

35 "Famed Medic of Cherokee To Talk Here," *Emmetsburg Democrat*, March 19, 1953: 1.

36 Drugs tested by Anthony A. Sainz on mental patients in state hospitals were reported in a wide range of psychiatric journals, conference proceedings, and newspaper articles, and referenced in some books on the history of mental illness treatments, including: "American Association for the Advancement of Science Meets," *Hospital Topics*, (1955) 33:3, 25-26; Febiger, Lee. "Chlorpromazine and Mental Health," *Proceedings of the Symposium Held Under the Auspices of Smith, Kline & French Laboratories.* June 6, 1955: 86; subsequently quoted in Whitaker, Robert. *Mad In America: Bad Science, Bad Medicine, and the Enduring Mistreatment of the Mentally Ill.* Cambridge, MA: (Perseus, 2002) 146; "Reserpine in the Treatment of Neuropsychiatric, Neurological, and Related Clinical Problems," *Annals of the New York Academy of Sciences*, Volume 61, (April 1955) 72–77; Sainz, Anthony, N. Bigelow, C. Barwise, and B. MacCasland., "Affective, changes produced by some phenothiazine and "diphenyl" derivatives in certain psychiatric syndromes," *Psychiatric Research Repairs*, American Psychiatric Association, (April 1958); Sainz, Anthony, N. Bigelow, and C. Barwise. "Rapid screening

of phrenopraxic drugs," *Psychiatric Quarterly* (April 1958) 32:2, 273-280; "Phenothiazines in the Management of Stress and Anxiety" *Psychosomatics*, Academy of Psychosomatic Medicine (1964) 5: 167-173; "Energy Drugs' May Balk Depression, " *Oakland Tribune*, August 3, 1958,on a meeting of the American Psychiatric Association in San Francisco; "New Marcy Facility to Pioneer in Research," *Observer Dispatch*, Utica NY, February 19, 1963; Shorter, Edward and Healy, David, *Shock Therapy: A History of Electroconvulsive Treatment in Mental Illness* (Rutgers University Press, NJ, 2007): 174.

37 Robert Whitaker, *Mad in America* (Perseus Books Group, New York, 2002) 143.

38 News headlines in 1969 from a variety of sources, including "Top News Stories from 1969," *infoplease.com*, "Summer of 1969," *CNN.com*, "What Happened in 1969," September 5, 2013 *www.thepeoplehistory.com*.

39 "Youth: The Hippies," *Time Magazine*, July 7, 1967.

40 Perphenazine is the generic name for the brand-name drug, Trilafon. September 7, 2013 http://www.drugs.com/dosage/perphenazine.html.

41 "Mental Health Spokesmen Say Cures Harder Than Thought," *Utica Daily Press*, October 5, 1966: 11.

42 *Drugs.com* September 7, 2013 http://www.drugs.com/mtm/trilafon.html..

43 For more information: http://www.drugs.com/cdi/perphenazine.html.

44 For more information: *http://www.drugs.com/ppa/methylphenidate-hydrochloride.html*.

45 Newspaper archives used in research: http://newspaperarchive.com/ and http://www.fultonhistory.com/Fulton.html.

46 "Famed Medic of Cherokee," *Emmetsburg Democrat*, March 19, 1953: 1.

47 "New Drug for Mental Patients," INS wire story published in *Waterloo Daily Courier*, December 30, 1954: 2.

48 Ray A. Wayne, Ph.D., and others, "Antipsychotics and the Risk of Sudden Cardiac Death," JAMA Psychiatry, December 2001, 58 (12): 1161-1167. Also, "Thorazine," Drugs.com September 8, 2013 http://www.drugs.com/cdi/thorazine.html.

49 "Iowa City Man in Talk Monday at Cedar Falls," *Waterloo Daily Courier*, March 4, 1955: 17.

50 Herman Bundensen, M.D., "Drug Quiets Irritability," *Mason City Globe-Gazette*, November 14, 1955: 14.

51 "Dr.Anthony Sainz Will Be Speaker," *Syracuse Herald Journal*, April 30, 1958: 48.

52 *Daily Sentinel*, Rome, NY, June 18, 1957: 5.

53 "Honored," Utica Observer-Dispatch, October 23, 1963: 44.

54 Dick Costa, "The Costa Living: War of Nerves," *Utica Observer Dispatch*, November 7, 1959: 8.

55 Bob Fensterer, "Marcy Research Team Closes in On 'New Cures'," *Utica Observer Dispatch* August 24, 1962: 13.

56 "New Marcy Facility to Pioneer in Research," *Utica Observer Dispatch*, February 19, 1963: 9.

57 "Sainz Chosen Head of Education Group," *Utica Observer Dispatch*, February 21, 1961: 12.

58 "Project MKULTRA: The CIA's Program of Research in Behavior Modification," Dark Matters, Science Channel, http://science.discovery.com/tv-shows/dark-matters-twisted-but-true/documents/project-mkultra.htm, accessed September 7, 2013. Also Kim Zetter's "This Day in Tech: April 13, 1953: CIA OKs MK-ULTRA Mind-Control Tests," Wired Magazine Online April 13, 2010, September 7, 2013 http://www.wired.com/thisdayintech/2010/04/0413mk-ultra-authorized/.

59 "MKULTRA." *The National Security Archive.* The George Washington University. Web. September 8, 2013 http://www2.gwu.edu/~nsarchiv/.

60 Email correspondence between the author and Mary Curry, Ph.D., Public Service Coordinator and Research Associate at The National Security Archive of George Washington University, April 27, 2009.

61 James L. Rupert, "Genitals to Genes: The History and Biology of Gender Verification in the Olympics", *Canadian Bulletin of Medical History*, Volume 28:2, 2011: 339-365. Also, Vanessa Heggie's, "Testing sex and gender in sports; reinventing, reimagining and reconstructing histories," Endeavour. 2010 December; 34(4): 157–163.

62 "New Marcy Facility to Pioneer in Research," *Utica Observer Dispatch*, February 19, 1963: 9.

63 Stuart A. Kirk and Herb Kutchins, "The Myth of the Reliability of DSM," *Academy for the Study of the Psychoanalytic Arts* September 8, 2013 http://www.academy-analyticarts.org/kirk&kutchins.htm. Also, Bruce Poulsen's, "Reality Play: Revisiting the Myth of Mental Illness: Some Thoughts on Thomas Szasz," *Psychology Today* September 17, 2012, September 7, 2013 http://www.psychologytoday.com/blog/reality-play/201209/revisiting-the-myth-mental-illness-some-thoughts-thomas-szasz.

64 "Doctors Favor Marcy Facility," *Daily Press* [Utica, NY] November 16, 1971.

65 "Jimmy Bremmer Killer May Be Tried in Le Mars: Blood Pools indicate Murder Occurred In Plymouth County," *Le Mars Globe Post* [Le Mars, Iowa] September 30, 1954: 1.

66 Rita Starzl and Glada Koerselman, "Order new Triplett trial here because of huge drug doses," Le Mars Daily Sentinel, October 17, 1972, Vol. 100, No. 207.

67 Robert Bartels, *Benefit of Law: The Murder Case of Ernest Triplett*, (Iowa State University Press, Ames, Iowa, 1988): 135. Bartels is a law professor who represented Triplett in legal proceedings to challenge his conviction.

68 Bartels, p. 109.

69 "Jimmy Bremmer Homicide," *Iowa Cold Cases, Inc.* describes itself as "a non-profit organization committed to providing case summaries, articles and updates for all Iowa open homicides and missing persons cases where foul play is suspected." September 5, 2013 http://iowacoldcases.org/case-summaries/jimmy-bremmers/.

70 *http://www.townofmarcy.org/content/History*. More on this hospital to prison transition in New York State can be found at http://www.correctionhistory.org/html/chronicl/docs2day/fishkill.html. More information on Utica State Hospital can be seen at a volunteer-driven wiki on asylums worldwide called *"Asylum Projects"* at: http://www.asylumprojects.org/index.php?title=Utica_State_Hospital and http://nysasylum.com/utica/index.htm.

71 Robert E. Doran, M.D., "History of Willard Asylum for the Insane and the Willard State Hospital" (1978, Original paper housed at New York State Library), 45.

WORKS CITED

"Agreement for UNRRA." *Pillars of Peace: Documents Pertaining To American Interest In Establishing A Lasting World Peace.* (1946): *Ibiblio.* Web. 3 Sep 2013. http://www.ibiblio.org/pha/policy/1943/431109a.html.

"American Association for the Advancement of Science Meets," *Hospital Topics* 33:3 (1955): 25-26. Print.

Bartels, Robert. *Benefit of Law: The Murder Case of Ernest Triplett.* Ames, Iowa: Iowa State University Press, 1988. 135. Print.

"Brain Surgery Is Performed at State Institute." *Cedar Rapids Gazette* 13 March 1953: 15. Print.

Bundesen, Herman. "Drug Quiets Irritability." *Mason City Globe-Gazette* 14 November 1955: 14. Print.

"Contributors to this issue: Anthony Sainz, M.D." *Psychiatric Quarterly.* 31.1-4 (January 1957): 190-197. Print.

Costa, Dick. "The Costa Living: War of Nerves." *Utica Observer Dispatch* 7 November 1959: 8. Print.

Cudmore, Bob. "Life in 1946." *Daily Gazette* 20 June 2009. Print.

Daily Sentinel [Rome, NY] 18 June 1957: 5. Print.

"Doctors Favor Marcy Facility." *Daily Press* [Utica, NY] 16 November 1971. Print.

Doran, Robert E., *History of Willard Asylum for the Insane and the Willard State Hospital.* New York State Library, 1978. 5-40. Print.

"Dorothea Lynde Dix." *History of Psychology Archives. Muskingum College's Psychology Program.* Web. 2 Sep 2013. http://www.muskingum.edu/~psych/psycweb/history/dix.htm.

"Dr. Anthony Sainz Will Be Speaker." *Syracuse Herald Journal* 30 April 1958: 48. Print.

"Dr. Wynegar to Leave Mental Health Institute." *Cedar Rapids Gazette* 25 July 1952: 11. Print.

"Famed Medic of Cherokee to Talk Here." *The Emmetsburg Democrat* 19 March 1953: 19. Print.

Febiger, Lee. "Chlorpromazine and Mental Health." *Proceedings of the Symposium Held Under the Auspices of Smith, Kline & French Laboratories* 6 June 1955: 86. Print.

Fensterer, Bob. "Marcy Research Team Closes in On 'New Cures'." *Utica Observer Dispatch* 24 August 1962: 13. Print.

Fox, Thomas C. "Vietnam's 400-year Catholic History." *National Catholic Reporter* 24 April 2003. Web. 15 Sep 2013. http://www.nationalcatholicreporter.org/today-stake/tt042403.htm.

Freeman, Walter. "Amygdaloidectomy for the suppression of auditory hallucinations; a preliminary report of a theory and its application in one case." *Medical Annals of the District of Columbia* (1951). Print.

Heggie, Vanessa. "Testing sex and gender in sports; reinventing, reimagining and reconstructing histories." *Endeavour* 34.4 (2010): 157–163. Print.

"Honored." *Utica Observer Dispatch* 23 October 1963: 44. Print.

"Iowa City Man in Talk Monday at Cedar Falls." *Waterloo Daily Courier* 4 March 1955: 17. Print.

"Jimmy Bremmer Homicide." *Iowa Cold Cases, Inc.* Web. 5 Sep 2013. http://iowacold-cases.org/case-summaries/jimmy-bremmers/.

"Jimmy Bremmer Killer May Be Tried in Le Mars: Blood Pools indicate Murder Occurred In Plymouth County." *Le Mars Globe Post* [Le Mars, Iowa] 30 September 1954: 1. Print.

"Just War Doctrine." *Catholic Answers to Explain and Defend the Faith*. Web. 5 Sep 2013. http://www.catholic.com/documents/just-war-doctrine.

Kirk, Stuart A., and Herb Kutchins. "The Myth of the Reliability of DSM." *Academy for the Study of the Psychoanalytic Arts*. Web. 8 Sep 2013. http://www.academyana-lyticarts.org/kirk&kutchins.htm.

Lightner, David L. *Asylum, Prison and Poorhouse: The Writings and Reform Work of Dorothea Dix in Illinois*. Illinois: Carbondale Edwardsville, Southern Illinois University Press, 1999. Print.

Mecomber. "The Old Main, or Utica Lunatic Asylum, NY." *New York Traveler* 29 Oct 2010. Web. 2 Sep 2013. http://newyorktraveler.net/the-old-main-or-utica-lunatic-asylum-ny/.

"Mental Health Conclave Set." *Evening Recorder* [Amsterdam, New York] 19 April 1958. Print.

"Mental Health Spokesmen Say Cures Harder Than Thought." *Utica Daily Press* 5 October 1966: 11. Print.

"Metrazol." *Fairfield State Hospital 1933-1995*. Web. 2 Sep 2013. http://www.fairfield-statehospital.com/metrazol.html.

"MKULTRA." *The National Security Archive*. George Washington University. Web. 8 Sep 2013. http://www2.gwu.edu/~nsarchiv/.

"New Drug for Mental Patients." *Waterloo Daily Courier* 30 December 1954: 2. Print.

"New Marcy Facility to Pioneer in Research." *Utica Observer Dispatch* 19 February 1963: 9. Print.

"Open Large-scale Surgery on State Mental Patients." *Council Bluffs Iowa Nonpareil* 20 July 1952: 24. Print.

"Our History." *City of Rome, NY.* Official Website of the City of Rome. Web. 15 Sep 2013.

Penney, Darby, and Peter Stastny. *The Lives They Left Behind: Suitcases from a State Hospital Attic.* The Willard Suitcase Exhibit Online [Belleview Literary Press, 2008.] Web. 2 Sep 2013. http://www.suitcaseexhibit.org/indexhasflash.html.

"Perphenazine." *Drugs.com.* Web. 7 Sep 2013. http://www.drugs.com/dosage/perphenazine.html.

Pflaum, George A. "This Godless Communism," *Treasure Chest of Fun & Fact* (1961). Comic book. *Catholic University of America Archives.* Web. 3 Sep 2013. http://archives.lib.cua.edu/findingaid/treasurechest.cfm.

Poulsen, Bruce. "Reality Play: Revisiting the Myth of Mental Illness: Some Thoughts on Thomas Szasz." *Psychology Today* 17 September 2012. Web. 7 Sep 2013. http://www.psychologytoday.com/blog/reality-play/201209/revisiting-the-myth-mental-illness-some-thoughts-thomas-szasz.

Project MKULTRA: The CIA's Program of Research in Behavior Modification. Dark Matters, Science Channel, Film. 7 Sep 2013. http://science.discovery.com/tv-shows/dark-matters-twisted-but-true/documents/project-mkultra.htm

"Public Invited on Tour of Cherokee State Hospital." *Le Mars Semi Weekly Sentinel* 29 May 1951: 2. Print.

"Reserpine in the Treatment of Neuropsychiatric, Neurological, and Related Clinical Problems." *Annals of the New York Academy of Sciences* 61 (1955): 72–77. Print.

Rome, NY Military On-Line Museum. Web. 5 Sep 2013. http://romemilitarymuseum.tripod.com/

Rupert, James L. "Genitals to Genes: The History and Biology of Gender Verification in the Olympics." *Canadian Bulletin of Medical History* 28.2 (2011): 339-365. Print.

Sainz, Anthony. "Dr. Sainz to Talk at County Public Health Dinner." The Laurens Inn [Laurens, Iowa] 22 April 1954. Speech.

Sainz, Anthony, N. Bigelow, and C. Barwise. "Rapid screening of phrenopraxic drugs." *Psychiatric Quarterly* 32:2 (1958): 273-280. Print.

Sainz, Anthony, N. Bigelow, C. Barwise, and B. MacCasland. "Affective, changes produced by some phenothiazine and 'diphenyl' derivatives in certain psychiatric syndromes." *Psychiatric Research Repairs, American Psychiatric Association,* 1958. Print.

"Sainz Chosen Head of Education Group." *Utica Observer Dispatch* 21 February 1961: 12. Print.

Sidel, Victor W. "Herbert Abrams in China: International Social Medicine." *Journal of Public Health Policy* 28.1 (2007): 165-180. *JSTOR.* Web. 3 Sep 2013.

Starzl, Rita, and Glada Koerselman. "Order new Triplett trial here because of huge drug doses." *Le Mars Daily Sentinel* 100.207 (1972). Print.

"Teachers Meet Here Wednesday." *Oelwein Daily Register* 30 October 1954: 8. Print.

The Lobotomist. PBS, 2008. Documentary. 5 Sep 2013. http://www.pbs.org/wgbh/americanexperience/films/lobotomist/player/.

"The Social Welfare History Project on Dorothea Lynde Dix." *Social Welfare History.* Web. 2 Sep 2013. http://www.socialwelfarehistory.com/people/dix-dorthea-lynde/

"Thorazine," *Drugs.com.* Web. 8 Sep 2013. http://www.drugs.com/cdi/thorazine.html

The Doors. "Break on Through (To the Other Side)," *The Doors.* Elektra Records, 1967. Vinyl.

Wagner, James R. *Wagner and Allied Families Scrapbook.* Family genealogical paper, 1998. 5-30. Print.

Wagner, Linda. "Cherokee Mental Health Institute, Iowa Department of Human Services." Message to Roxanne Moller. 17 February 2009. E-mail.

Wagner, Linda. Message to Mary Curry, Ph.D., Public Service Coordinator and Research Associate at The National Security Archive of George Washington University. 27 April 2009. E-mail.

Wayne, Ray A., Ph.D., and others. "Antipsychotics and the Risk of Sudden Cardiac Death," *JAMA Psychiatry* 58: 12 (2001): 1161-1167. Print.

Whitaker, Robert. *Mad In America: Bad Science, Bad Medicine, and the Enduring Mistreatment of the Mentally Ill.* Cambridge, MA: Perseus, 2002. 146. Print.

Whitbourne Ph. D., Susan Krauss. "Fulfillment at Any Age – Mindlessness and Memory Slips: How to Find What You've Lost." *Psychology Today Online* 25 January 2011. Web. 4 Sep 2013. www.psychologytoday.com.

"Youth: The Hippies." *Time Magazine.* 7 July 1967. Print.

Zetter, Kim. "This Day in Tech: April 13, 1953: CIA OKs MK-ULTRA Mind-Control Tests." *Wired Magazine Online* 13 April 2010. Web. 7 Sep 2013. http://www.wired.com/thisdayintech/2010/04/0413mk-ultra-authorized/.

AUTHOR PHOTO BY SHEILA WINETT

Linda Mary Wagner spent more than a dozen years as an independent journalist, primarily for National Public Radio and its member stations in Buffalo and Chicago. She later worked as a communications specialist for The Brooklyn Historical Society, Consumers Union, and Associated Press. While earning her Masters in Public Administration from Columbia University, she forged a third career in nonprofit leadership and management. Currently employed as a non-profit executive in the public health field in Albany, New York, Ms. Wagner is married and the mother of two adult children.

Unearthing the Ghosts: A Mystery Memoir is her first book.